From Contented Baby
to Confident Child

From
Contented Baby
to
Confident Child

Problem-solving in the
first three years

Gina Ford

Vermilion
LONDON

To my beloved mother and best friend
in blessed remembrance of all her wisdom, the very special love,
support and encouragement she always gave me
and who taught me the difference between right and wrong
and how always to march to the beat of my own drums.

First published in the United Kingdom in 2000 by Vermilion
an imprint of Ebury Press
Random House, 20 Vauxhall Bridge Road,
London SW1V 2SA

Random House Australia (Pty) Limited
20 Alfred Street, Milsons Point, Sydney
New South Wales 2061, Australia

Random House New Zealand Limited
18 Poland Road, Glenfield,
Auckland 10, New Zealand

Random House (Pty) Limited
Endulini, 5A Jubilee Road, Parktown 2193,
South Africa

The Random House Group Limited Reg. No. 954009
www.randomhouse.co.uk

A CIP catalogue record for this book
is available from the British Library

ISBN 0 09 187523 4

Printed and bound in Great Britain by
Biddles Ltd, Guildford and King's Lynn

Papers used by Vermilion are natural, recyclable products made from
wood grown in sustainable forests.

Contents

Acknowledgements

In writing this book, I have relied enormously on the continual feedback from and the constant contact with hundreds of parents who have shared their babies with me. It has been both a great honour and a privilege that they have continued to involve me in their family life for many years after I first went to help care for their babies.

I would like to thank all of those parents and in particular the following whose constant encouragement, enthusiasm and invaluable suggestions have made this book possible: Katy and Simon Brewer, Verity and Michael Chambers, Jackie and Andrew Marr, Sabrina and Danny Masri, Amelia and Neil Mendoza, Helen and David Sherbourne and Catherine and Rupert Vaughan Williams.

My editor Joanna Carreras has yet again done a great job in transforming my manuscript into an understandable and readable text. She deserves not only a thankyou but an OBE for her endless patience regarding my rather chaotic approach to writing.

I owe a further debt of thanks to the following people who have not only helped me hugely with my books but whose emotional support, encouragement and friendship gave me the strength to fulfil my beloved mother's dying wish for me to have two books published. My dear cousin Sheila Eskdale and my friends Janetta and Keith Hodgson, Jane Revell, Juliette and Alistair Scott and Francoise and Steven Skelley.

A very very special debt of thanks also goes to my Aunt Jean and Uncle Dan who, despite having four children of their own as well as six grandchildren and five great-grandchildren, have always found the time to love, help and support me in every way possible since the death of my beloved mother on November 10th 1998.

Finally, I would like to thank the thousands of readers of *The Contented Little Baby Book* who have contacted me; your letters and telephone calls of support mean more to me than you will ever know.

Foreword

I am sure that critics of my first publication *The Contented Little Baby Book* will be horrified that I have had the temerity to write a follow-on book. Two months prior to publication of *Contented Baby to Confident Child* a review appeared on a website from a mother announcing my forthcoming book which she believed 'should make interesting reading, even if we do ignore all her advice'. Like so many who are opposed to my views on demand feeding she failed to grasp the real facts. The main one is that for a huge number of parents demand feeding leads to long-term feeding and sleeping problems. Another critic, a health visitor, also voiced her strong professional objections on the internet saying that she had discussed my book with colleagues and had yet to find anyone who would recommend it to a mother. She chose to ignore the fact that 38 out of the 44 reviews on the website came from parents who said how my book had been a godsend and changed their life. Babies who had previously been fed on demand became much happier and more content since following my advice and routines.

I appreciate that there always has been and always will be different views on styles of parenting, and would stress that my books are specifically written for parents who believe that babies and children benefit from routine. Over the last few years it has become extremely fashionable for experts to cite Third World practises as the ideal way to bring up babies and children. Feeding babies on demand and sleeping with them is supposed to result in a closer bond between baby and parents. However, having lived and worked in several Third World countries and seen these practises first-hand, I believe the authors of such books over-romanticise the reality and do little to help parents who are trying to raise confident children who can cope in the Western world.

Contented Baby to Confident Child, like my first book, is based on my experience of working and living with many different families and observing first-hand what works and what doesn't. It has been written in response to the thousands of letters and calls I have received from parents requesting a follow-on to my first book. Its aim is to help parents recognise the many different stages that their child goes through during the first three years of life, helping them to use their common sense and instinct when dealing with old-age problems.

Like my first book it focuses much on feeding and sleeping as I believe that both of these things have a great influence on the behaviour and wellbeing of babies and young children. A well-nourished and well-rested child will find it much easier to cope with the many challenges he faces during his early years than a child who is under-nourished and overtired.

I hope that the advice in this book will go some way towards helping parents feel more relaxed and knowledgeable, enabling their 'contented baby' to become a 'confident child'.

Just one final point – for clarity I have followed the same style as in my first book and, where relevant, the mother is always 'she', the father is always 'he' and the baby is always 'he'.

1

Feeding problems in the first year

When I ask parents what was the most difficult aspect of parenting in the first year, the majority of them will say sleep – or rather the lack of it. The number of phone calls I receive from anxious parents experiencing problems with their young babies consistently confirms this. A disruptive sleeping pattern is nearly always top of the list of worries they wish to discuss. When they give details of their baby's feeding and sleeping habits, I usually find that the disrupted nights are very often a result of incorrect feeding.

Regardless of whether they are breast feeding or bottle feeding, these mothers have nearly always followed the current advice given by healthcare officials and fed their babies on demand. For many mothers, and especially first-time mothers, this means feeding their baby every time he cries, often every two hours right around the clock. The experts reassure these parents that feeding the baby whenever he cries and for as long as he wants is the best way to deal with excessive crying. Parents tell me that they were never advised to look for other reasons why their baby might be crying.

The majority of parents put their faith in these experts, accepting the advice that these difficult times are part and parcel of parenting – and will eventually pass. Like thousands of other parents, they continue to struggle along exhausted and miserable, believing the advice that an erratic feeding pattern is normal in young babies, and that they will eventually fall into a more regular feeding pattern.

Sadly, from my past experience with young babies who are milk fed on demand, this is very rarely the case. The thousands of phone calls and letters I have received from parents since my first book was published can confirm this. The majority are from parents desperate for advice on how to deal with an older baby or toddler who refuses to eat, and who is often still waking in the night. The root of the problem nearly always stems back to the lack of structure in milk feeding in the very early days.

Milk feeding: how things go wrong

As they grow, all babies will increase the amount they drink. However, the feeds must be structured to coordinate a baby's growth, thereby encouraging him to take more milk at individual feeds. If not, he will be very likely to continue to feed little and often. All too often I get calls from the parents of older babies who are still following the demand rules of milk feeding. While the majority of these babies are over 12 weeks and are physically capable of drinking more at individual feeds, they continue to feed as they did as new-borns – often between eight and ten times a day.

Many of the breast-fed babies are still having only one breast at each feed, while bottle-fed babies may only be taking 90–120ml (3–4oz) of formula. In order to go for longer spells between feeds, these babies should be taking from both breasts at each feed, or have a formula feed of 210–240ml (7–8oz). It is my firm belief that it is during those early days of milk feeding that the foundation is laid for healthy eating habits in the future. To avoid long-term feeding problems that also can affect your baby's sleep, it is advisable to structure and solve any milk feeding problems early on.

Breast feeding: low milk supply

Not producing enough milk, especially later in the day, is a very common problem for breast-feeding mothers. I believe that hunger is one of the main reasons why so many babies are fretful and difficult to settle in the evening. If the problem of a low milk supply is not resolved in the early days then a pattern soon emerges of the baby needing to feed on and off all evening to try and satisfy his needs. Mothers are advised that this constant feeding is normal and the best way to increase the milk supply, but in my experience it usually has the opposite effect. Because the amount of milk the breasts produce is dictated by the amount of milk the baby drinks, these frequent feeds signal the breasts to produce milk little and often. These small feeds will rarely satisfy the baby, leaving him hungry and irritable.

I believe that the stress involved in frequently feeding a very hungry, irritable and often overtired baby can cause many mothers to become so exhausted that their milk supply is reduced even further. Exhaustion and a low milk supply go hand in hand, and are the main reasons why so many mothers give up breast feeding. I am convinced that by expressing a small amount of milk during the early weeks of breast feeding, when the breasts are producing more milk than the baby needs, the mother can help avoid the problem of a low milk supply.

If your baby is under one month of age and not settling in the evening it is possible the cause is a low milk supply. Expressing at the times suggested in the routines laid out in my first book should help solve this problem. The short amount of time you will spend expressing will ensure that during any future growth spurts you will be producing enough milk to meet immediately any increase in your baby's appetite. If your baby is over one month and not settling in the evening or after day-time feeds the following six-day plan will quickly help to increase your milk supply. The temporary introduction of top-up feeds will ensure that your baby is not subjected to hours of irritability and anxiety caused by hunger, which is what usually happens when mothers resort to demand feeding to increase their milk supply.

Plan for increased milk supply

Days one to three

6.45am

- Express 30ml (1oz) from each breast.
- Baby should be awake, and feeding no later than 7am regardless of how often he fed in the night.
- He should be offered 20–25 minutes on the fullest breast, then 10–15 minutes on the second breast.
- Do not feed after 7.45am. He can stay awake for up two hours.

8am

- It is very important that you have a breakfast of cereal, toast and a drink no later than 8am.

9am
- If your baby has not been settling well for his nap offer him 5–10 minutes on the breast from which he last fed.
- Try to have a short rest when the baby is sleeping.

10am
- **Baby must be fully awake now, regardless of how long he slept.**
- He should be given 20–25 minutes from the breast he last fed on while you drink a glass of water and have a small snack.
- Express 60ml (2oz) from the second breast, then offer him 10–20 minutes on the same breast.

11.45am
- He should be given the 60ml (2oz) that you expressed to ensure that he does not wake up hungry during his midday nap.
- It is very important that you have a good lunch and a rest before the next feed.

2pm
- **Baby should be awake and feeding no later than 2pm regardlesss of how long he has slept.**
- Give him 20–25 minutes from the breast he last fed on while you drink a glass of water. Express 60ml (2oz) from the second breast, then offer 10–20 minutes on the same breast.

4pm
- Baby will need a short nap according to the routine appropriate for his age.

5pm
- **Baby should be fully awake and feeding no later than 5pm.**
- Give 15–20 minutes from both breasts.

6.15pm
- Baby should be offered a top-up feed of expressed milk from the bottle. A baby under 8lb in weight will probably settle with 60–90ml (2–3oz), bigger babies may needs 120–150 (4–5oz).
- Once your baby is settled it is important that you have a good meal and a rest.

8pm
- Express from both breasts.

10pm
- It is important that you express from both breasts at this time, as the amount you get will be a good indicator of how much milk you are producing.
- Arrange for your husband or another family member to give the late feed to the baby so you can have an early night.

10.30pm
- Baby should be awake and feeding no later than 10.30pm. He can be given a full feed of either formula or expressed milk from a bottle. Refer to the chart on page 9 for details of the amounts to give.

In the night
A baby who has had a full feed from the bottle at 10.30pm should manage to get to 2–2.30am in the morning. He should then be offered 20–25 minutes from the first breast, then 10–15 minutes from the second. In order to avoid a second waking in the night at 5am it is very important that he feeds from both breasts.

If your baby fed well at 10.30pm and wakes earlier than 2am the cause may not be hunger. The following checklist gives other reasons which may be causing him to wake earlier.

- Kicking off the covers may be the cause of your baby waking earlier than 2am. A baby under under six weeks who wakes up thrashing around may still need to be fully swaddled. A baby over six weeks may benefit from being half swaddled under the arms in a thin cotton sheet. With all babies it is important to ensure that the top sheet is tucked in well, down the sides and at the bottom of the cot.
- The baby should be fully awake at the 10pm feed. With a baby who is waking up before 2am it may be worthwhile keeping him awake longer, and offering him some more milk just before you settle him at around 11.30pm.

Day four
By day four, your breasts should be feeling fuller in the morning and the following alterations should be made to the above plan.

- If your baby is sleeping well between 9am and 9.45am reduce the time on the breast at 9am to five minutes.

- The top-up at 11.45am can be reduced by 30ml (1oz) if he is sleeping well at lunch time, or shows signs of not feeding so well at the 2pm feed.
- The expressing at the 2pm feed should be dropped, which should mean your breasts are fuller by the 5pm feed.
- If you feel your breasts are fuller at 5pm, make sure he totally empties the first breast before putting him onto the second breast. If he has not emptied the second breast before the bath he should be offered it again after the bath, and before he is given a top-up.
- The 8pm expressing should be dropped and the 10pm expressing brought forward to 9.30pm. It is important that both breasts are completely emptied at the 9.30pm expressing.

Day five

- Dropping the 2pm and 8pm expressing on the fourth day should result in your breasts being very engorged on the morning of the fifth day; it is very important that the extra milk is totally emptied at the first feed in the morning.
- At the 7am feed the baby should be offered 20–25 minutes on the fullest breast, then 10–15 minutes on the second after you have expressed. The amount you express will depend on the weight of your baby, as it is important that you take just the right amount so that enough is left for your baby to get a full feed. If you managed to express a minimum of 120ml (4oz) at the 10pm feed, you should manage to express the following amounts:

  a) baby weighing 8–10lb – express 120ml (4oz)
  b) baby weighing 10–12lb – express 90ml (3oz)
  c) baby weighing over 12lb – express 60ml (2oz)

Day six

By the sixth day, your milk supply should have increased enough for you to drop all top-up feeds, and follow the breast-feeding routine laid out in my first book that is appropriate for your baby's age. It is very important that you also follow the guidelines for expressing as set out in the routines. This will ensure that you will be able to satisfy your baby's increased appetite during his next growth spurt. I would also suggest that you continue with one bottle of either expressed or formula milk at the 10pm feed until your baby is weaned onto solids at four months. This will allow the feed to be given by your husband or partner, enabling you to get to bed earlier, which in turn will make it easier for you to cope with the middle of the night feed.

Expressing

I have always believed that expressing a small amount of milk during the early weeks of breast feeding can help avoid the problem of a low milk supply. The enormous feedback from mothers who followed the routines in my first book is further evidence of this. Those mothers who followed my guidelines for expressing in the very early days, rarely experienced the problem of a low milk supply and very quickly established a regular feeding pattern. When their babies went through growth spurts every few weeks, the routine stayed intact, because any increased appetite could be immediately satisfied simply by expressing less milk at the early morning feeds. These babies continued to have a steady weight gain and gradually slept longer from the last feed, eventually going from 11pm–6–7am.

Unfortunately, the mothers who followed the routines but excluded the expressing were faced with a problem when their baby went through a growth spurt and needed extra milk. These mothers found they had to go back to feeding two- or three-hourly, and often twice in the night to increase their milk supply. This pattern of feeding was repeated each time their baby went through a growth spurt and made it very difficult to keep the routine going. Feeding two-hourly, more often than not, resulted in the baby being fed to sleep, and created a further problem of the wrong sleep association. Expressing is an excellent way of increasing a low milk supply and keeping the baby in a routine. If done from the very early days it can help to avoid altogether the problem of a low milk supply.

If you have previously experienced difficulties with expressing, do not be disheartened. Expressing at the times suggested in my routines or the plan on page 13, along with the following guidelines should help make it easier.

- The best time to express is in the morning as the breasts are usually fuller. Expressing will also be easier if done at the beginning of a feed. Either express one breast just prior to feeding your baby, or feed your baby from one breast, then express from the second breast before offering him the remainder of his feed. Some mothers actually find that expressing is easier if done while they are feeding the baby on the other breast.

- In the early days, you will need to allow at least 15 minutes to express 60–90ml (2–3oz) at the morning feeds, and up to 30 minutes at the evening expressing times. Try to keep expressing times quiet and relaxed. The more you practise the easier it will become. I usually find that by the end of the first month the majority of my mothers can easily express 60–90ml (2–3oz) within five minutes at the morning feeds, and 180–240ml (6–8oz) within ten minutes at the 10pm feed.

- An electrical, heavy-duty expressing machine, the type used in hospitals, is by far the best way to express milk in the early days. The suction of these machines is designed to stimulate a baby's sucking rhythm, encouraging the milk flow. If you are expressing both breasts at 10pm it is also worthwhile investing in an attachment that enables both breasts to be expressed at once, therefore reducing the time spent expressing.

- Sometimes the let down is slower in the evening when the breasts are producing less milk; a relaxing warm bath or shower will often help encourage the milk to flow more easily. Also gently massaging the breasts before and during expressing will also help.

- Some mothers find that it is helpful to have a picture of their baby close by for them to look at, while others find it better to watch a favourite television programme or to chat to their partners or husbands. Experiment with different approaches to see which one works best for you.

Formula: overfeeding

Unlike the breast-fed baby the most common problem in the early days with formula-fed babies is overfeeding. The reason I believe this can happen with some babies is that they take the bottle of formula so quickly that their natural sucking instincts are not satisfied and they end up screaming when the bottle is removed from their mouth. Many mothers interpret this cry as one of hunger and end up giving them another bottle of formula. A pattern of overfeeding can quickly emerge, resulting in the baby gaining huge amounts of weight each week. If this problem is allowed to continue the baby quickly reaches a stage where milk alone will not satisfy his appetite, yet he is too young to be given solids.

While it is normal for some babies to need an 30ml (1oz) at some feeds, special attention should be given if a baby is taking in excess of 150ml (5oz) every day, and is regularly gaining more than 24ml (8oz) each week. When my formula-fed babies show signs of being particularly 'sucky' I have found that offering some cool boiled water between feeds and a dummy afterwards helps to satisfy their sucking needs.

If you are concerned that your baby is overfeeding it is essential that you discuss the problem with your health visitor or doctor.

A baby under four months will need 70ml (2½oz) of milk for each 1lb of his body weight over a 24–hour period. Occasionally a very hungry baby may need an extra 30ml (1oz) at some feeds. Try to ensure that this is given at the late evening feeds, rather than the middle of the day feeds. For example a baby given an extra 30ml (1oz) at the 2pm feed may take less at the 6.15pm feed. This can result in him waking earlier for the 10pm feed, which has a knock-on effect of him waking earlier in the night.

The following guidelines give the approximate amount of formula a baby needs each day during the first four months of his life.

Weight	Daily amount	Number of feeds in 24 hours
6lb	450ml (15oz)	7 – 8
7lb	540ml (18oz)	6 – 7
8lb	600ml (20oz)	6 – 7
9lb	690ml (23oz)	6 – 7
10lb	750ml (25oz)	5 – 6
11lb	840ml (28oz)	5 – 6
12lb	900ml (30oz)	5 – 6
13lb	990ml (33oz)	5
14lb	1.05l (35oz)	5
15lb	1.14l (38oz)	4 – 5

Difficult feeder

The majority of newborn babies take to the breast or bottle quickly and easily. Unlike the new mother who has much to learn about feeding, the baby instinctively knows what is expected of him. However, there are some babies who from day one will fuss and fret within minutes of being put on the breast or being offered the bottle. I often find that some babies who have undergone a particularly difficult birth can be more difficult to feed.

If you find that your baby becomes tense and fretful at feed times try to avoid having visitors at such times. No matter how well-meaning family and friends may be, it will be impossible to keep things completely calm and quiet if you are having to make conversation.

The following guidelines, regardless of whether your are breast or bottle feeding, should help make feeding your tense baby easier.

- It is essential that the handling of these tense babies is kept to the minimum. Avoid overstimulation and handing the baby from person to person, especially before a feed.
- The feed should be given in a quiet room with a calm atmosphere. Apart from perhaps one person to offer practical help and emotional support, no other person should be allowed in the room.
- Prepare everything needed for the feed well in advance. Try and make sure that you have rested and have eaten.
- Avoid turning on the television during a feed, unplug the telephone and play some calm music while feeding.
- When the baby wakes for his feed, do not change his nappy as this may trigger off crying. It is very important to prevent the baby becoming tense before a feed.
- Try swaddling him firmly in a soft cotton sheet to prevent him thrashing his arms and legs around. Make sure that you are comfortable before you start feeding.
- Do not attempt to latch the baby onto the breast or put the bottle straight in his mouth if he is crying. Hold him firmly in the feeding position and calm him down with continuous gentle patting on the back.

- Try holding a dummy in his mouth. Once he has calmed down and has sucked steadily for a few minutes, then very quickly ease the dummy out and offer him the breast or the bottle.

If your baby has been feeding well and suddenly starts to refuse the breast or bottle, it could be because he is feeling unwell. Ear infections can easily go undetected and are a very common cause of a baby not wanting to feed. If your baby shows any of the following signs it would be advisable to consult your doctor.

- Sudden loss of appetite, and becoming upset when offered a feed
- Disruption to the normal sleep pattern
- Suddenly becoming clingy and whingey
- Becomes lethargic and unsociable

Mixed feeding

Many mothers attempt to try a combination of breast feeding and formula feeding, especially if they have to cope with a new baby and a very young, demanding toddler. If successful, it can enable a busy mother to give a bottle feed to the baby at those times of the day when she is trying to meet the different demands of elder brothers and sisters. However, I have found that those mothers who attempt to do mixed feeding before they have established a good breast milk supply can very quickly end up with a totally formula-fed baby. I believe that the main reason for this is not nipple confusion, as many of the experts claim, but the fact that breast milk and formula milk are digested very differently.

A baby under six weeks will not work so hard at emptying the breast if a previous day-time feed was a bottle of formula which takes longer to digest. Because the baby demands less milk the breasts soon start producing less. A vicious circle quickly emerges, as the breasts produce less milk and the baby then needs to drink more formula at the alternate bottle feed.

If you want to avoid this, it is important that you structure the introduction of formula feeds very carefully. My plan for mixed feeding, which has worked well for many mothers, is divided into stages and should be used in conjunction with the routine suitable for your baby's age. The plan, along with the guidelines below needs to be followed very carefully if you wish the combination of breast feeding and formula feeding to be a success.

- The long-term success will depend very much on making sure that in the early days the breast receives enough stimulation to establish a milk supply.
- It is also important to remember that it takes around 6–8 weeks to build up a good milk supply. The same principles of a healthy diet and rest should still apply, even if you decide not to breast feed exclusively.
- The key to building up a good milk supply, which is essential for mixed feeding and a routine, is the total emptying of the breasts at 10pm using a double pumping expressing machine. The plan is unlikely to work if another time is substituted for the expressing.
- The amount you express will serve as a good indicator to how much you are producing. In my experience, a mother who expresses 90–120ml (3–4oz) at 10pm and feeds the baby once in the night will usually produce double that amount in the morning.
- The first formula feed should always be at the 10pm feed. Formula milk is digested more slowly than breast milk, and should therefore always be given at a time you want the baby to have a longer spell between feeds.
- I would not advise introducing a second formula feed until your baby is at least four weeks old. If you are expressing a minimum of 90–120ml (3–4oz) of milk at 10pm, then you can introduce a further bottle feed using the milk you express at 10pm. This bottle of expressed milk should be given at either the 10am or 2pm feed – but never at both.
- Introducing two expressed feeds during the day before six weeks can lead to your baby rejecting the breast.
- If too many bottles are introduced before the breast milk supply is established, then long-term mixed feeding is less likely to be successful.

Plan for combined
breast and formula feeding

Stage one

7am
• Breast feed and express according to routine.

10am
• Breast feed and express according to routine.

2pm
• Breast feed according to routine.

5pm
• Breast feed according to the routine – a baby over 8lb should be offered both breasts.

6.15pm
• Bottle feed using milk expressed in the morning.

10pm
• Bottle feed of formula can be given by father allowing mother to express and get to bed early.

In the night
Breast feed according to the routine and offer the second breast if your baby is waking regularly before 7am.

Stage two

Once your baby reaches four weeks of age and weighs over 8lb you can proceed to Stage two, provided you are expressing 90–120ml (3–4oz) at 10pm. With a bigger baby who feeds quickly and is emptying both breasts at most feeds, it may be possible to advance to Stage two sooner. An indicator that this is happening will be that his weekly weight gain is good and he settles well between day-time feeds and sleeps five hours or more from his 10pm feed.

7am
• Breast feed and express according to the routine.

10–11am
• Breast feed or bottle of expressed milk.

2pm
- If you breast fed at the last feed, this feed can be either a breast feed or a bottle of expressed milk.
- If the last feed was a bottle feed it is essential that this feed is from the breast.

5pm
- Breast feed according to the routine – a baby over 8lb in weight should be offered both breasts.

6.15pm
- Bottle of expressed milk.

10–11pm
- Bottle of formula can be given by your husband or partner while you express from both breasts.

In the night
Breast feed according to routine. If your baby is waking regularly before 7am make sure he feeds well from both breasts.

Stage three

When your baby reaches eight weeks of age and weighs over 12lb you can proceed to Stage three, and drop the 5pm feed, provided his weekly weight gain is good and he is settling well in between feeds. The amounts expressed in the morning should have been reduced in accordance with the advice given in the breast-feeding routines, until they are eventually dropped altogether.

The 10pm expressing should be continued if you wish to keep giving expressed milk at one of the bottle feeds. If you decide to drop the 10pm expressing and your baby is sleeping through the night, it would be advisable to do so by gradually reducing the amount expressed, to avoid the possibility of engorgement.

7am
- Breast feed according to routine.

10–11am
- Bottle of expressed milk or formula.

2pm
- Bottle of expressed milk or formula.

6.15pm
- Breast feed according to routine.
- A baby who weighs over 12lb and is not settling may need a top-up feed of expressed milk or formula.

10–11pm
- Bottle feed of formula.
- Expressing – optional.

In the night
Breast feed according to routine; offer the second breast if your baby is waking regularly before 7am in the morning. If your baby is feeding in the night and then sleeping through to 7am and is cutting back on his morning feed, try gradually to decrease the length of time he feeds from the breast in the night.

Excessive night feeding

I believe that by the end of the second week a baby who weighed 7lb or more at birth should really only need one feed (between midnight and 6am) in the night. This is provided, of course, that he is feeding well at all of his day-time feeds and gets a full feed between 10pm and 11pm. In my experience, regardless of whether they are breast or bottle fed, a baby who continues to feed two or three times in the night will eventually begin to cut back on his day-time feeds. A vicious circle soon emerges, where the baby cuts back so much on his day-time feeds that he ends up genuinely needing to feed in the night so that his daily nutritional needs can be met.

With bottle-fed babies it is easier to avoid a pattern of excessive night-time feeding evolving by monitoring the amounts they are getting during the day. The chart on page 9 gives details of how much milk a formula-fed baby would need to satisfy his daily nutritional needs. Following these guidelines along with the ones about the core night (page 17) will prevent excessive night feeding for a formula-fed baby.

Excessive night-time feeding is considered normal for breast-fed babies and is actually encouraged by many breast-feeding experts. Mothers are advised to have their baby sleep with them, so that he can feed on and off throughout the night. Much emphasis is placed on the fact that the hormone prolactin, which is necessary for making breast milk, is produced more at night. The theory is that mothers who feed their babies more in the night than in the day, are much more likely to sustain a good milk supply. This advice obviously works for some mothers, but breast-feeding statistics prove that it clearly doesn't for many others as so many give up in the first month.

I believe that the exhaustion caused by so many night-time feeds is one of the main reasons why so many mothers give up breast feeding.

In my experience from working with hundreds of breast-feeding mothers, I have found that a good stretch of sleep in the night results in the breasts producing more milk. A full and satisfying feed in the middle of the night will ensure that the baby settles back to sleep quickly until the morning.

The following guidelines give the main causes of excessive night-time feeding and how it can be avoided.

- A premature baby or a very tiny baby would need to feed more often than three-hourly, and medical advice should be sought on how best to deal with these special circumstances.
- If he feeds well at every feed (a baby over 8lb should always be offered the second breast) and is sleeping well at all the other sleep times, he may not be getting enough from the 10–11pm feed.
- If a low milk supply at the last feed is the problem, it can easily be solved by ensuring your baby takes a full feed from a bottle of either formula or expressed milk. If you decide to offer expressed milk, you will need to allow enough time to express for the feed, which can be added to milk from the morning expressing.
- Many women are concerned that introducing a bottle too early may reduce the baby's desire to take the breast. All of my babies are offered one bottle a day as a matter of course and I have never had one baby who had nipple confusion or refused the breast. It also has the added advantage that the father can give the last feed and enable the mother to get to bed slightly earlier.
- If after one week of giving a full feed at this time there is no improvement, and your baby still is waking several times a night or more, it is more likely that your baby has a problem with his sleeping than with his feeding. I suggest that you con-

tinue to offer the bottle for a further week and refer to page 44 in Chapter 2 for more advice on night waking.

- Babies under 8lb in weight who are changed to the second breast before reaching the fatty, rich hind milk in the first breast will be more likely to wake more than once in the night.

- If a baby weighs over 8lb in weight at birth and is only feeding from one breast at a feed, then he may not be getting enough milk, and should be offered the second breast at some or all of his feeds. If he has fed for 20–25 minutes on the first breast then try to get him to take 5–10 minutes from the second. If he refuses, try waiting 15–20 minutes before offering it again.

Dropping the 2am feed

The routines in *The Contented Little Baby Book* along with the above guidelines should quickly help to reduce the number of feeds your baby is having in the night to only one feed, and encourage him to go for a longer spell from his last feed. I have found that all babies, even demand-fed babies, are capable of sleeping one longer spell between feeds by the time they reach 4–6 weeks of age. Beatrice Hollyer and Lucy Smith, authors of an excellent book called *Sleep – The Secret of Problem-free Nights*, describe this longer stretch of sleep as the 'core night'. They advise parents to take their cue from the core night, which they believe is the foundation of encouraging a baby to sleep right through the night.

The majority of the babies on my routines who are only feeding once in the night gradually push themselves right through the night, dropping the middle of the night feed as soon as they are physically capable. However, occasionally I get a baby who reaches six weeks and continues to wake at 2am looking for a feed. In my experience, allowing these babies to continue to feed at this time usually results in them reducing the amount they take at 7am, often cutting this feed out altogether. When this happens I would use the core night method to ensure that when the baby is ready to reduce the number of feeds he is having over a 24–hour period, it is always the middle of the night feed that he drops first.

The core night

The method called the 'core night' has been used for many years by maternity nurses and parents who believe in routine. It works on the principle that once a baby sleeps for one longer spell in the night, he should never again be fed during the hours slept in the course of the core night. If he wakes during those hours, he should be left for a few minutes to settle himself back to sleep. If he refuses to settle, then other methods apart from feeding should be used to settle him. Hollyer and Smith recommend patting, offering a dummy or giving a sip of water. Attention should be kept to the minimum while reassuring the baby that you are there. They claim that following this approach will, within days, have your baby sleeping at least the hours of his first core night. It also teaches the baby the most important of two sleep skills: how to go to sleep, and how to go back to sleep after surfacing from a non-REM (rapid eye movement) sleep.

Dr Brian Symon, author of *Silent Nights* and a senior lecturer in general practice at the University of Adelaide, recommends a similar approach for babies over six weeks. Babies who are putting on a good amount of weight each week, but who are still waking at 3am should be offered the dummy or some cool boiled water. If the baby refuses to settle then give the shortest feed possible that will allow him to settle.

Neither of these methods of dealing with night feeding are new in babycare. Babycare expert Christine Bruell, who has advised over 35,000 mothers during her 40–year career, also advises offering cool boiled water to a thriving baby over four weeks of age if he keeps regularly waking at 2am.

Before embarking on these methods the following points should be read carefully to make sure that your baby really is capable of going for a longer spell in the night.

- These methods should never be used with a very small baby or a baby who is not gaining weight. A baby not gaining weight should always be seen by a doctor.
- The above methods should only be used if your baby is regularly gaining 180–240ml (6–8oz) each week, and if you are sure that his last feed is substantial enough to help him sleep for the longer stretch in the night.
- The main sign that a baby is ready to cut down on a night feed is a regular weight gain and the reluctance to feed, or feed less at 7am in the morning.
- The aim of using any of the above methods is gradually to increase the length of time your baby can go from his last feed and not to eliminate the night feed in one go.

- The core night method can be used if over three or four nights a baby has shown signs that he is capable of sleeping for a longer stretch.
- It can be used to try and reduce the number of times a demand-fed baby is fed in the night and to encourage a longer stretch between feeds, or after his last day-time feed.

Breast feeding and returning to work

If you are planning to return to work and would like to continue to breast feed, it is important that you try to make sure that you have established a good milk supply, especially if you want your baby to have expressed milk during the day. A three-month baby will need two feeds of approximately 210–240ml (7–8oz) each of expressed milk if you are out between 9am and 5pm. As your baby will most likely be emptying both breasts at the 7am and 6pm feed, you will need to express most of the milk for the feeds to be given in your absence during the working day or between 9pm and 10pm in the evening.

You should fit in two expressings at around 10am and 2.30pm. If you express any later than this it is possible that your breasts will not produce enough for the 6pm feed, especially if you are in a hurry to get home.

The following guidelines give suggestions on how to incorporate working and breast feeding.

- The longer you can spend at home establishing a milk supply the easier it will be to maintain it once you return to work. Most breast-feeding experts advise a period of 16 weeks.
- Expressing from the beginning of the second week at the times suggested will enable you to build up a good stock of breast milk in the freezer.
- Introducing a bottle of expressed milk at the 10pm feed by the second week will ensure that there will not be a problem of your baby not taking the bottle when you return to work.
- Check with your employer well in advance of returning to work that there will be a quiet place available where you will be able to express. Also check that they are happy for you to store the expressed milk in the refrigerator.
- Once you have established a good expressing routine using the heavy duty expressing pump you should begin practising with

a battery operated one. With a single expressing pump you may find that switching from side to side throughout the expressing will help the milk to flow easier. It may also be worthwhile considering a mini-electric pump that will enable you to express both breasts at once.

- Make sure that your nanny or child-minder is familiar with the storage and handling of breast milk, and how to defrost it.
- Establish the combined feeding routine that you will be using for your baby at least two weeks in advance of your return to work. This will allow you plenty of time to sort out any difficulties that may occur.
- Once you return to work it is essential that you pay particular attention to your diet and that you rest well in the evening. It would be advisable to continue expressing at 10pm to ensure that you continue to have a good milk supply. Also make sure that you keep a good supply of breast pads at work, and a spare shirt or top!

Shaun: aged six months

Shaun was exclusively breast fed from birth, apart from one formula feed at 10pm, and he happily followed the routines in my first book from the age of two weeks. Although Shaun's mother had never expressed at the times I suggested, Shaun was sleeping through the night to 7am from his 10pm feed at the age of eight weeks. He started solids at four months and because she was planning to return to work part-time when Shaun was six months she also introduced a bottle of formula at the 2pm feed. He was very reluctant to take the bottle and would never drink more than 90ml (3oz). However, his weight gain was still good and he continued to sleep from 7pm–7am. At six months when his mother returned to work, she introduced protein at his 11.30am feed and dropped the milk. Shaun was now having a breast feed at 7am and 6.30pm, and a bottle of formula at 2.30pm. Within a week of the new feeding pattern commencing Shaun began waking up at 5am. His mother attempted to settle him back to sleep by patting him or offering him water, but this rarely worked. Such an early start to the day resulted in Shaun being very grumpy and overtired by the time his mother returned home from work at 5pm.

When I received Shaun's feeding chart it was obvious that the reason for his 5am waking was one of genuine hunger caused by the sudden drop in his daily milk intake. I believed that there were two reasons for the reduction in his milk intake. The first was that, unlike most babies, Shaun did not automatically increase the amount he drank at his 2.30pm feed when the 11.30am feed was dropped. The second reason was that his mother's milk supply had decreased very rapidly when she started work and went down to two feeds a day. This meant that in addition to the too small feed at 2.30pm, Shaun was also not getting enough milk at the 6.30pm feed, resulting in a genuine need to feed at 5am.

Unfortunately, because Shaun had been given a bottle so infrequently and refused to drink a top-up after the 6.30pm feed, and because he was only taking the smallest amount from a bottle at 2.30pm, his mother had to continue to feed him at 5am.

When she eventually decided to wean him completely on to formula feeds, I suggested that she should first replace the morning feed with a bottle, before the evening one. Because Shaun had gone for a longer spell without food he would be less likely to fight the bottle. Once he was totally weaned on to formula he started to sleep through until 7am again.

I believe that this problem could have been avoided if his mother had continued to express at 9.30–10pm in the evening, which would have helped keep up her milk supply. Also, because she knew she was returning to work it would have been better to get Shaun used to taking a full feed from a bottle at a much earlier stage.

Breast-fed babies: excessive wind

A breast-fed baby does not normally take in as much air as a bottle-fed baby and may not always bring up wind after a feed. If your baby has not brought his wind up within a few minutes but still seems happy, it is best not to spend ages trying to get the wind up, as the endless rubbing and patting on the back can actually cause more upset than the wind itself. A baby who is genuinely bothered by wind will scream and scream after a feed – nothing will console him until he manages to burp.

The following guidelines should be observed if your baby is showing signs of excessive wind.

- I have found that babies who are positioned incorrectly on the breast are more likely to be bothered with wind. Frequently I observe mothers holding their babies as if they were bottle feeding. This means the baby is not able to latch on to the breast properly, which results in him taking in more air than necessary. It is worthwhile arranging a home visit from your health visitor or your NCT breast-feeding counsellor, who will teach you how to position your baby on the breast correctly.

- If you are confident that you are holding your baby properly, and that he is positioned correctly on the breast, the wind may be caused by something you are eating. Occasionally some babies react to certain foods that their mother has eaten, and the pain usually occurs 12–16 hours after the mother has eaten the offending food.

- The main foods I have found to cause a reaction in babies, if eaten in excess, are dairy products, citrus fruits, mushrooms and tomatoes. While tea, coffee, sugar and chocolate do not appear to cause wind, I do find that if taken in excess they can cause irritability in some babies. If you suspect a certain food may be causing your baby's wind, trying cutting out that particular food for several days. If there is a marked improvement, wait a further week before introducing the food again, and even then do so gradually. However, if you find that even the smallest amount of the suspect food causes your baby excessive wind, I would advise that you discuss this with your health visitor or doctor.

- It is essential that a breast-feeding mother eat a varied and healthy diet and consume an extra 500 calories a day. Try to avoid too many convenience foods that are loaded with additives and empty starches. This is not a time for diet or excessive exercise; losing weight too quickly will not only reduce the amount of milk you produce, but could also result in the toxins that are accumulated in the fatty tissue being released into your breast milk. Some experts believe these toxins can cause irritability in babies.

Bottle-fed babies: excessive wind

While babies who are bottle fed tend to take in more wind than breast-fed babies this should not create a problem, so long as the baby is given the opportunity to burp once during the feed and once at the end. It is often assumed that burping a bottle-fed baby after every ounce will result in the baby taking in less wind. I have not normally found this to be the case, and more often than not I find that the baby gets distressed because the bottle is constantly being removed from his mouth. If your bottle-fed baby has problems in bringing up his wind which leaves him in a lot of discomfort, the first thing you should look at is the amount of formula your baby is taking and how often he is feeding. A formula-fed baby needs 75ml (2½oz) of formula per 1lb of his body weight each day. Refer to the chart on page 9 to determine if you are feeding your baby the correct amounts. I believe that overfeeding is one of the major causes of excessive wind. Occasionally, a very hungry baby may need a little more a day, but if your baby is drinking 150ml (5oz) or more in excess of the recommended daily amount, then he may be overfeeding and this can cause severe wind pains.

The following guidelines may be of some help if you find your baby is suffering from excessive wind.

- If you are sure that your baby is taking the right amount of formula for his weight, the next thing to look at is the type of bottle and teat you are using. I certainly find that the wide-necked bottle designed by Avent with its specially designed teat helps reduce the amount of air a baby takes in.
- Pay extra attention when making up the formula feed; follow the manufacturer's instructions to the letter and make sure that you shake the bottle well, then shake it again to make sure the water and powder are thoroughly mixed together.
- Before feeding your baby, loosen and rescrew the ring and teat back on to release any excess air. Ensure that you keep the bottle tilted so that the teat is filled with milk at all times. Keeping the baby in a more upright position during and after feeding also helps reduce the amount of air he takes in.
- Laying the baby flat on his back for a couple of minutes, then slowly raising him to a sitting position may help release trapped air. Alternatively, lay the baby flat on his tummy with his head to one side, while gently rubbing his back.
- Some parents find that colic drops such as Infacol help their baby's excessive or trapped wind. There are also natural alter-

natives like Chamomilla drops or Windypops, which contain camomile, fennel, catnip and lemon balm. Whether using conventional or alternative treatments it is always advisable to discuss the correct dosages with a health visitor or qualified homeopath.

Weaning worries

The current advice to parents is to start introducing solids to their babies between the age of four and six months, and to establish a pattern of three proper meals a day between the age of six and nine months. By the age of one year a baby is expected to be eating much the same food as the rest of the family, and taking all drinks from a cup.

From the calls and letters I receive, and from reading many problem pages in baby magazines, it is obvious that a great many parents are struggling to meet these guidelines. All of these concerned parents are looking for answers to their babies' or toddlers' poor eating habits. I am convinced that the majority of these feeding problems stem from the current advice given by many experts that during the first few months of a baby's life he should be allowed to take the lead with milk feeding. The people giving this advice seem to ignore the fact that a great number of babies will, if allowed, continue to feed little and often long past an age when they are capable of taking larger feeds and going for longer spells between them.

In my experience, babies who reach four months and are still milk feeding on demand, regardless of whether they are breast or bottle fed, will have a much more difficult time in reaching a pattern of three meals a day, which is what is expected of them by the time they reach 6–9 months. The problems regarding solid food may vary considerably during the first year, but I believe that regardless of their age, the problem is nearly always related to milk – either too much or too little of it.

Refusal of solids

With babies five months or older, the refusal of solids is often caused because they drink too much milk, especially if they are still feeding in the middle of the night. Every day I speak to parents of babies and toddlers who will barely touch solids, let alone eat three meals a day. In the majority of these cases the babies are still being milk fed on demand, some feeding as often as two or three times in the night. While milk is still the most important food for babies under six months, failing to structure the time of milk feeds and the amounts given can seriously affect the introduction of solids. If your baby is refusing solids, the following guidelines will help you determine the cause.

- The recommended age to introduce solids is between four and six months. If your baby is under five months, gaining weight well and sleeping through the night from his 10pm feed, he simply may not be ready to be weaned yet.
- A baby is ready to be weaned when he shows signs that his appetite is no longer satisfied with 4–5 full milk feeds a day. A full milk feed is either a formula feed of 240ml(8oz) or a feed from both breasts.
- If your baby reaches four months and is having five full feeds a day, and still having a milk feed in the middle of the night he will be less inclined to want solids during the day. Gradually reducing the amount of milk he is taking in the night will encourage his interest in solids.
- If your baby is over five months, taking five full milk feeds a day and refusing solids, I would suggest discussing with your health visitor about gradually reducing one of the milk feeds, to encourage his interest in solids. If he has to be woken at 7am in the morning I would advise cutting back gradually on the 10pm feed using the method I recommend in my first book. If he is waking earlier than 7am I would suggest that you cut back on the 11am milk feed instead so as to encourage him to take solids then. Once he is happily taking solids at 11am, introduce some after the 6pm feed. As his appetite increases, so will the amount of solids he takes, which will have a knock-on effect of him drinking less at the 10pm feed.
- If your baby reaches six months and is having more than four full milk feeds a day his refusal of solids is certainly caused by drinking too much milk. It is important to cut right back on his 11am milk feed to encourage him to eat more solids at that time. By the end of six months a baby's milk intake should be around 600ml (20oz) a day, divided between three drinks a day and small amounts used in food. If your baby is still refus-

ing solids at this age, despite cutting down on his milk intake, it is important that you discuss the problem with your doctor or health visitor.

David: aged seven months

David, who was bottle fed from birth, would wake up screaming every hour and a half in the night, and was fretful and miserable for most of the day. When he was three months old, his exhausted parents decided to buy The Contented Little Baby Book. *They later admitted to being both suspicious and sceptical about my advice and techniques, which contradicted all the other books they had consulted. However, as the other advice hadn't worked, desperation led them to follow my routines to the letter. Within three days David was sleeping through the night and had become a happy and contented baby during the day. This pattern continued for two months.*

Then, when David outgrew his Moses basket at five months of age, his parents decided that they would move his twenty-month-old sister Andrea into a bed and give her cot to David. He continued to sleep well when moved to the big cot, but the move from the cot to a bed for Andrea turned out to be a disaster and resulted in weeks of hysterical crying and sleepless nights for her.

While the situation with Andrea was becoming steadily worse, exhaustion led her mother to neglect David's diet and routine. He was just given jars of baby food rather than the fresh food which had been an essential part of his dietary requirements. She also started to cut out his bath and massage in the evening. Soon David started waking every night at 10pm for a feed which he had dropped a good six weeks back and, worse still, he would be woken by his sister's cries in the night. His mother ended up by giving him a formula feed in the night so that he would settle quickly and allow her to return to an hysterical Andrea.

This excessive night-time milk feeding resulted in David eating even fewer solids than usual. He would take only a small amount of cereal after his morning bottle, the equivalent of two cubes of vegetables at lunch time, and two teaspoonfuls of baby rice at teatime. This amount of solids was too small and did not include any form of protein, which is essential for a baby aged seven months and weighing nearly 17lb.

Although she was exhausted trying to deal with two sleepless children, David's mother followed my advice and made two batches of lentil and vegetable casserole and two batches of chicken and vegetable casserole. Within two days of introducing this food at lunch time David began to drink less in the night. She gradually increased his lunch-time solids to six cubes of chicken or lentil casserole, and his teatime baby rice and fruit from two teaspoonfuls to six teaspoonfuls. These amounts were much more realistic for a baby of David's age and weight. Although he did continue to wake around 10pm for a further four nights, because his appetite was being satisfied during the day his mother managed to settle him back to sleep quickly without feeding him. Very soon David was back to sleeping soundly from 7pm–7am.

I believe that the main cause of David waking and wanting to feed in the night was due to him not receiving the correct amounts of the right sorts of food during the day. In my experience the occasional use of convenience food is fine, but babies who are being fed consistently from jars and packets are much more likely to develop sleeping problems related to feeding.

Milk refusal

The amount of milk a six-month-old baby drinks will gradually begin to reduce as his intake of solid food increases. However, up to the age of nine months a baby still needs a minimum of 500–600ml (18–20oz) a day of breast or formula milk. This daily amount gradually reduces to a minimum of 350ml (11½oz) at one year of age. If your baby is losing interest or refusing some of his milk feeds and taking less than the recommended amounts, careful attention should be given to the timing of solids and the type of food given.

The following guidelines will help you determine the cause of your baby refusing his milk feeds.

- Up to the age of six months a baby should still be taking a full milk feed morning and evening. A full milk feed consists of 210–240ml (7–8oz) or a feed from both breasts. Babies under six months who are given solids in the middle of their milk feed will be more likely to refuse the remainder of their formula or the second breast.

- A baby under five months of age still needs a full milk feed at 11am in the morning. Introducing breakfast too soon or offering too much solid food first thing in the morning can cause a baby to cut down too quickly or to refuse the 11am feed.
- The 11am milk feed should be reduced gradually between the ages of five and six months. Introducing the tier system of feeding (when you alternate between milk and solids during a feed) before five months can also be the reason a baby refuses his milk at this feed.
- Giving lunch-time solids at 2pm and evening solids at 5pm is the reason many babies under six months cut down too quickly or refuse their 6pm milk feed. Until he reaches six months it is better to give a baby his lunch-time solids at 11am and his evening solids after he has had a full milk feed at 6pm.
- Giving hard-to-digest foods such as banana or avocado at the wrong time of the day can cause a baby to cut back on the next milk feed. Until a baby reaches six months it is better to serve these types of food after the 6pm feed, rather than during the day.
- Babies over six months of age who begin to refuse milk are often being allowed too many snacks in between meals or too much juice. Try replacing juice with water and cutting out snacks in between meals.
- Between nine and twelve months some babies begin refusing the bedtime milk feed, which is a sign that they are ready to drop their third milk feed. If this happens it is important to reduce the amount given at the 2.30pm feed, before eventually dropping it altogether.

Tara: aged 5½ months

Tara was breast fed on demand for the first seven weeks of her life. It was nearly four weeks before she regained her birthweight, and at six weeks her weekly weight gain was so low that her mother was advised to top up after each feed with formula milk. By seven weeks she was getting virtually all her feeds from the bottle. Her mother had breast fed her other two children for three months, and as she was keen to do the same for Tara, she contacted me for advice. I suggested that she follow my plan for a low milk supply for one week.

Because her milk supply was so low, I advised that she would have to top up with formula after the 10.30am feed, instead of expressed milk, as the plan suggests. Within one week her milk supply had increased so much that Tara was taking the breast at all the day-time feeds, with a top-up of expressed milk after the 10.30am and 6.15pm feeds. She continued to have one formula feed at 11pm and by the end of the 8th week Tara was happily in the 6–8 week routine, and sleeping through to 7am from her last feed. Tara continued to feed well from the breast and gained 240ml (8oz) in weight each week until she was three months old. At this stage her mother gradually began to introduce more formula milk and by four months Tara was on four full formula feeds a day and sleeping from 7pm–7am.

Things continued to go well for a further six weeks until one night Tara suddenly woke up at 2am. Her mother was concerned that she might genuinely be hungry as she had only taken 150ml (5oz) at the 6pm feed, so she offered her a small 120ml (4oz) feed. Tara drank this quickly but still refused to settle back to sleep, until she was given a further 120ml (4oz) of formula. She then settled back to sleep very quickly and had to be woken at 7am.

During the following week Tara became more and more difficult over her day-time milk feeds, and a pattern soon emerged of her only taking 120–150ml (4–5oz) at each of her day-time feeds, and only 90–120ml (3–4oz) at 6.15pm, before waking up desperately hungry between 2am and 3am. When her mother contacted me for advice she assured me that she was still following my routines and guidelines to the letter. The daily records she sent me showed that the structure and timing of milk feeds and solids were correct. However, she had decided to introduce certain foods that are more difficult to digest earlier than I recommended. Banana, which I advise to introduce at six months was added to her breakfast cereal at five months. Tara loved banana, and this prompted her mother to offer it to her regularly at lunch time along with mashed avocado, another food that is hard to digest.

Tara's mother had allowed her to take the lead with weaning, which meant she cut back too quickly on her daily milk intake. As a result she was having to wake in the night to make up for the milk she was no longer getting during the day. It was clear from the feeding charts that the Tara, who then weighed 15lb, had cut back too dramatically on her milk intake during the day, because her solids had been increased too rapidly (especially at breakfast). This in turn affected the amount of milk she was taking at lunch *time. I advised her mother to cut back the breakfast cereal to two teaspoonfuls, with one or two cubes of pear or peach purée, instead of five teaspoonfuls of breakfast cereal and mashed banana. Lunch, which also consisted of hard-to-digest fruits such as banana and avocado, was replaced by 4–6 cubes of vegetable purée, made up of a combination of potato and choice of other vegetables from the ones suggested in the feeding charts found in my first book. After the 6pm milk feed I suggested that she be given 4–6 teaspoonfuls of baby rice mixed with two cubes of fruit purée, instead of vegetable purée.*

Within three days, Tara was back to sleeping from 7pm–7am. This problem of milk underfeeding was caused by introducing too much of the wrong types of food too early or at the wrong time. This is a very common mistake, and is the main reason for babies under six months cutting back too quickly on their day-time milk, which results in a genuine need to feed in the night.

Fussy feeder

If milk feeding is structured properly during the early days of weaning, the majority of babies will happily eat most of the foods they are offered. By the time they reach nine months babies are expected to be getting most of their nourishment from eating three solid meals a day. Parents are advised to offer their babies a wide variety of foods to ensure they receive all the nutrients they need. However, it is often around this time that many babies start to reject food they have previously enjoyed.

If your baby is between nine and twelve months of age and suddenly starts to reject his food, or becomes fussy and fretful at mealtimes, the following guidelines should help determine the cause.

- Parents often have unrealistic expectations of the amounts of food their baby should have and serving too large portions can mislead them into thinking that their baby has a feeding problem. The following list showing the amounts of food a baby aged between nine and twelve months of age needs will help you decide if your baby is eating enough solids.
    - ○ 3–4 servings of carbohydrate, made up of cereal, wholemeal bread, pasta or potatoes. A serving is one slice of bread, 25g

(1oz) of cereal, two tablespoonfuls of pasta, or a small baked potato.

○ 3–4 portions of fruit and vegetables, including raw vegetables. A portion is one small apple, pear or banana, carrot, a couple of cauliflower or broccoli florets, or two tablespoons of chopped green beans.

○ one portion of animal protein or two of vegetable protein. A portion is 25g (1oz) of poultry, meat or fish or 50g (2oz) of lentil and pulses.

- Self-feeding plays an important role in a baby's mental and physical development as it encourages hand-eye coordination and increases his sense of independence. Between six and nine months of age most babies will start to pick up their food and try to feed themselves. The whole business of feeding can become very messy and mealtimes take much longer. Restricting a baby's natural desire to explore his food and feed himself will only lead to frustration and very often refusal to be spoon fed. Introducing lots of finger foods and allowing him to eat part of his meal by himself regardless of the mess he makes will make him much more inclined to take the remainder from you off a spoon.

- By the time a baby reaches nine months of age he will become more interested in the colour, shape and texture of his food. A baby who is still having all the different foods mashed up together will quickly begin to get bored with even his favourite foods and is one of the main reasons that babies lose interest in vegetables.

- Offering your baby a selection of vegetables of various textures and colours at each meal in small amounts will be more appealing to him than a large amount of just one or two vegetables.

- Sweet puddings and ice-cream desserts served on a regular basis are major causes of babies and toddlers refusing their main course. Even babies as young as nine months can quickly learn that if they refuse the savoury foods and fuss enough, they will more than likely be given the pudding. It is better to restrict puddings and desserts to special occasions, and serve your baby fresh fruit, yoghurt or cheese as a second course.

- If your baby rejects a particular food it is important that he should be offered it again a couple of weeks later. Babies' likes and dislikes regarding food fluctuate a good deal in the first year and parents who fail to keep reintroducing food that is rejected usually find that their baby ends up eating a very restricted diet.

- Giving large amounts of juice or water prior to a meal can result in a baby not feeding very well. Try to offer him drinks midway between meals, not an hour before. Also at mealtime encourage him to eat at least half of the solids before offering him a drink of water or well-diluted juice.
- The timing of meals also plays a big part in how well a baby eats. A baby who is having his breakfast solids later than 8am, is unlikely to be very hungry for his lunch much before 1pm. Likewise a baby who is having tea-time solids later than 5pm may be getting too tired to eat well.
- Giving too many snacks in between meals especially hard-to-digest foods like bananas or cheese, can often take the edge off a baby's appetite. Try restricting snacks for a couple of days to see if his appetite improves at meal times.
- If you are concerned that your baby is not taking enough solids it is advisable to seek advice from your health visitor or doctor. Keeping a diary for a week, listing the times and amounts of all food and drinks consumed will help them to determine the cause of your baby's feeding problems.

Asha: aged nine months

Asha weighed nearly 10lb at birth and went straight into the 2–4 week routine. She breast fed well during the day, and slept through the night at four weeks after her formula feed at 10pm. She continued to sleep and feed well, following the routines to the letter until she was nearly nine months. It was at this stage that her parents rang me for advice, as things were going seriously wrong with Asha's feeding. Between eight and nine months of age she went from being an enthusiastic eater to being a fretful and fussy eater, refusing even her most favourite dishes.

As she had always been one of my favourite babies I immediately went to spend the day with her to try and sort out the problem. When I arrived Asha was playing; she was crawling well and had developed good hand-eye coordination, using the pincer grip (see page 33) to pick up and examine many of her smaller toys. She particularly enjoyed her shape-sorter toys, attempting to fit the various shapes into the appropriate holes, and got very cross when her mother attempted to help her find the correct hole. Asha's behaviour showed she was clearly very advanced both mentally and physically and had a very independent streak.

This independent streak became more obvious during lunch. From the minute Asha was placed in her high chair she started to get fussy and fretful and would shake her head from side to side when her mother attempted to feed her. With a struggle her mother managed to get Asha to take half of the food in the bowl, which to my surprise was still of a mashed consistency. Asha's mother had always followed my book to the letter, therefore I was intrigued to find out why she had not followed my advice of introducing chopped food by the age of nine months. She explained that she had tried this at seven months, but Asha's keeness to self-feed meant lunch ended up taking nearly 45 minutes instead of the usual 30 minutes. This meant Asha would go down for her midday nap later which resulted in her becoming overtired and not sleeping so well.

Once Asha was settled for her nap, I explained to her mother that self-feeding plays an important part in helping a baby develop physical and mental skills, by encouraging hand-eye coordination, and improving their fine finger control, often referred to as the pincer grip. Asha was encouraged to learn all these things during her play-time, then suddenly restricted at meal times, which must have caused her much confusion and frustration. At this age babies become very aware of colour and texture, and I am sure that Asha had become very bored with all her food being mashed up into one bowl.

For her tea that day I suggested that we prepare a selection of cubed vegetables with small pasta shapes and allow Asha to feed herself. There was much grabbing and squeezing of the food, and the meal certainly was more messy and took longer than usual, but Asha happily ate everything that was put in front of her. Because she had been allowed to satisfy her feelings of independence, she happily allowed her mother to spoon feed her the yoghurt and fruit that followed.

Once a baby starts to participate in feeding themselves it is important to allow extra time for their meals. I advised Asha's mother to bring her lunch forward by 15 minutes allowing a longer time until her self-feeding skills had improved.

2

Sleeping problems in the first year

Since the publication of my first book I have been contacted by hundreds of parents about their babies' sleeping problems. They confirm what I have always believed: it is the lack of routine that is the major cause of fretfulness and irritability in young babies and the main reason for sleeping problems during the first year. All of these parents were following current advice from health officials, feeding the baby on demand and allowing him to find his own sleeping pattern. They trusted the advice that it is impossible to implement a routine for a baby under three months of age.

Within a few weeks these parents were exhausted, anxious and feeling inadequate and frustrated as they struggled to cope with their sleepless baby. Sleep deprivation and desperation led them to buy *The Contented Little Baby Book*, often going against their health visitor's advice that it belonged in the dustbin! My methods are still frowned upon by a vast number in the medical profession, despite the fact that thousands of parents can testify how much happier and contented their baby is since following my advice and routines. The view of these childcare experts remains the same: that it is normal for young babies to wake several times a night.

However, just as trends in fashion change, so do trends in babycare. The enormous amount of research in America and Australia into sleeping habits of babies and young children confirms what our parents and grandparents have always known: babies and children are happier and cope with life better when in a routine. I also believe it is what a great many parents now want. If I needed further evidence of the pendulum swinging back to parents favouring routine, the response to my recent articles in *The Daily Telegraph* and *Evening Standard* provide powerful proof. Phone lines were jammed for several days when thousands of parents who share my beliefs rang to order my book.

The huge response from parents all over the world who are successfully following my advice goes even further to confirm my belief that a baby who is healthy and well fed is capable of sleeping for one longer stretch from an early age and that the majority of sleeping problems can be avoided.

Dr Symon (see page 18), shares my belief that parents should strive towards developing and encouraging a routine during the first six weeks. He also stresses the importance of monitoring daytime sleep to ensure that the long stretch of sleep is at night.

In his book *Silent Nights*, Dr Symon says that a baby aged between six and seven weeks who is feeding and growing well is strong enough to sleep at night for one long block of sleep of seven hours after the last feed. By eight weeks this can be extended to eight hours. Between three and six months he says most babies are capable of sleeping from 7pm–7am, although some may still need to feed briefly at the parents' bedtime. He believes that good quality sleep is as essential as good nutrition for healthy development of young babies, especially during the first few weeks. He says there is some evidence that sleep deprivation can slow and impair brain development because the immature and growing brain of the baby has a greater requirement for sleep than the mature brain. It's his belief that overhandling the baby after feeding times is a potential cause of overtiredness. The overtired baby can't and won't go to sleep and cries long and vigorously.

If your baby is difficult to settle in the evening or wakes more than once in the night it is important that you get a clearer understanding of his sleeping needs. Once you understand why things are going wrong, with the help of my advice and routines you will be able to help your baby establish a healthy sleep pattern.

Sleep cycles

Sleep is divided into two cycles called REM (Rapid Eye Movement) sleep usually referred to as light sleep, and non-REM sleep, usually referred to as deep sleep. A new-born baby goes straight into REM sleep when he first goes to sleep. During this light sleep his breathing becomes irregular, his body may twitch or jerk, his eyelids will flicker and his eyes appear to roll. He may even smile or frown during this cycle of light sleep. This sleep is often described as active sleep because a baby uses more oxygen and energy than during non-REM sleep. A baby who has gone full term will spend 50 per cent of his sleep cycle in REM sleep. A premature baby will spend 80 per cent. The rest of the sleep cycle is spent in non-REM sleep.

During non-REM sleep the baby's breathing will be slow and regular. There are no eye movements and only the occasional twitch or jerk of the body during this deep sleep. This calm sleep cycle is often described as quiet sleep. It allows the baby's mind and body to recharge, enabling him to cope with his next awake period. Research also shows us that this deep sleep is essential for the healthy development of a baby's mental and physical growth.

Dr Richard Ferber says in his bestselling book *Solve Your Child's Sleep Problems*, that non-REM sleep is well formed at birth but has not developed the four distinct stages experienced by older children and adults. It is not until the second month that a sequence of non-REM sleep stages begins to develop. When a baby of three months is ready to sleep, he first enters Stage one of non-REM – a drowsy sleep – then quickly passes into Stage two – a light sleep – before reaching Stages three and four – very deep sleep. This whole non-REM cycle lasts around 40–50 minutes. The baby then passes to the REM sleep cycle, which usually last 5–10 minutes, before returning to another cycle of non-REM sleep.

I believe that many parents begin to experience problems with their baby's day-time sleep once these different stages of non-REM sleep begin to develop. A baby under one year still needs one longer stretch of sleep in the middle of the day to avoid becoming overtired and fractious in the afternoon. If he is used to sleeping in a bright room, he may become fully awake after 45 minutes when he enters REM sleep. The day-time atmosphere makes it difficult for him to get into his next cycle of non-REM sleep. Parents sense that their baby is still tired and resort to feeding, rocking, patting, etc to help get him back to sleep.

What starts out to be a day-time sleep problem soon becomes a night-time sleep problem. The baby who needs assistance to return to sleep when he comes into a light sleep during the day will eventually come to need the same help at night. All babies and children come into a light sleep several times a night. This can mean several wakings for parents who have not helped their baby learn how to resettle himself back to sleep when he enters light sleep.

Day-time sleep

Parents always ask me what it is I do with my babies in the night to get them to sleep so well. My answer is always the same: very little. It is my experience that how a baby sleeps at night is very much dictated by how he feeds and sleeps during the day. I am convinced that the majority of sleeping problems are created in the very early days. To ensure that your baby sleeps well at night-time, it is essential that you structure his day-time sleep. Too much day-time sleep can result in several night-time wakings. Too little day-time sleep can result in his becoming overtired and irritable. He will have difficulty settling himself to sleep and will fall asleep only when he is totally exhausted.

Dr Marc Weissbluth, a leading researcher, paediatrician and director of the Sleep Disorders Center, Children's Memorial Hospital, Chicago, has conducted extensive research into the nap patterns of more than 200 children. In his book *Healthy Sleep Habits, Happy Child* he says that: 'Napping is one of the health habits that sets the stage for good overall sleep.' He explains that a nap offers the baby a break from stimuli and allows it to recharge for further activity. Charles Schaefer, PhD, professor of psychology at Fairleigh Dickinson University in Teaneck, New Jersey, supports this research and says: 'Naps structure the day, shape both the baby's and the mother's moods and offer the only opportunity for the mother to relax or accomplish a few tasks.'

Several other leading experts on childcare are in agreement that naps are essential to a baby's brain development. John Herman PhD, infant sleep expert and associate professor of psychology and psychiatry at the University of Texas, says: 'If activities are being scheduled to the detriment of sleep, it's a mistake. Parents should remember that everything else in a baby's life should come after sleeping and eating.'

This research confirms what I have always believed. Poor quality day-time sleep can affect not only the baby's mental development but also his ability to sleep well at night. This is further evidence to support my view of the importance of day-time sleep being established at the right time. The best time for the biggest nap of the day is between 12 noon and 2pm since this coincides with the baby's natural dip in alertness. A nap at this time will be deeper and more refreshing than a nap that starts later in the day.

It also plays a crucial part in establishing long-term healthy sleep habits in young babies and children.

Summary of day-time sleep between 7am and 7pm

Morning nap

A baby under one month of age is usually ready for a nap one and a half to two hours from the time he wakes up in the morning. By the time babies reach two months of age most will manage to stay awake the full two hours. If a baby stays awake longer than two hours he will often become overtired and fight sleep. Overtiredness is one of the main causes of a baby not settling well at nap time, and care should be taken that this does not happen. By the time they reach six months the majority of babies can stay awake for nearly two and a half hours. All babies should be woken no later than 10am if you want them to sleep for a longer time at 12noon.

At around one year of age most babies will cut right back on their morning nap, usually cutting it out altogether somewhere between 15 and 18 months.

Lunch-time nap

A baby under one month is often ready for this nap around 11.30am but by the time he reaches two months he can usually make it to 12noon. Ideally this should be the biggest nap of the day as recent research shows that a nap between 12noon and 2pm is deeper and more refreshing than a later nap, because it coincides with the baby's natural dip in alertness. Once a baby reaches six months of age and his morning nap becomes later, the lunch time nap will also come later – usually around 12.30pm.

Depending how well the baby has slept at the morning nap this nap usually lasts between 2 to 2½ hours. At around one year of age this may be cut back to 1½ hours if the baby is still having a full 45 minute nap in the morning, although it may lengthen again to two hours once the morning nap is dropped. The majority of babies will continue to need a nap at midday until they are two years of age, at which time they will gradually reduce the amount of time they sleep, cutting it out altogether somewhere between 2½ to three years of age.

Late afternoon nap

If a baby sleeps well at the two earlier naps in the day this should be the shortest of the three naps. A baby under eight weeks usually needs between 30 minutes to one hour. By the time they reach 12 weeks of age the majority of babies who have slept well at lunch time will only need a very short nap of 15 to 20 minutes in order to revive them enough for the bath and bedtime routine. This nap is usually dropped somewhere between three and six months of age. Allowing a baby to have a long sleep later in the day is often the reason a baby does not settle well at 7pm.

The total amount of daily sleep your baby has between 7am and 7pm will play a big part in how well he sleeps at night. The timings of the sleep is also important if overtiredness is to be avoided. Listed below is an approximate guide to the number of hours of nap time a baby under one years needs.

- Birth to four weeks – 5 hours
- Four to eight weeks – 4 to 4½ hours
- Eight to twelve weeks – 3½ hours
- Three to six months – 3 hours
- Six months to 12 months – 2½ to 3 hours

Harriet: aged three months

Harriet weighed over 9lb at birth and happily went straight into the two to four week routine. She followed the routines like clockwork during the day and had regularly slept though the night from three weeks of age. Her parents called me when she was over four months in total despair because she had started to wake up several times a night and was irritable and unhappy during the day.

Things started going wrong when she was around three months, which coincided with the time a nanny was employed. The nanny began to lengthen the time of Harriet's morning nap and to cut back on her lunch-time nap so that they could attend various play dates in the afternoon.

The shorter lunch-time nap meant that Harriet started to get tired and irritable in the late afternoon. The bath and bedtime routine quickly went from being a happy and relaxing event to a very tearful one. Harriet's parents insisted that her naps were changed back to the original times. Unfortunately, despite cutting the morning nap back to 40 minutes, Harriet would fully awaken from her light sleep during the lunch-time nap and not resettle. They tried feeding her, giving her the dummy, nothing worked. Eventually they tried leaving her to cry but she got so distressed that they ended up picking her up after 20 minutes. This went on for a couple of weeks and the parents had more or less resigned themselves to the fact that they had lost the long lunch-time sleep. Then to their horror Harriet started to wake up several times at night. Every time she came into a light sleep, she would cry until one of her parents went in and helped her settle back to sleep. That was when they decided to call me for help.

I explained that in order to get Harriet back to sleeping well at night we would also have to sort out her day-time sleep. I believed it was essential for Harriet to learn to settle herself back to sleep when she surfaced from light sleep 45 minutes into her lunchtime nap.

On the first day of sleep training, when Harriet came into her light sleep I advised the parents to wait 10-15 minutes before checking her. They could then go in for two or three minutes and stroke her forehead and say, 'Ssh, shh' but under no circumstances were they to talk to her or pick her up. She cried on and off for the remaining hour of her lunch-time nap. She woke twice in the night for 40–45 minutes each time and the parents used the same approach as during the day.

The following day I advised them to wait 20–25 minutes before going in to her at the lunch-time nap and the same in the night-time. She cried for much the same time during the lunch-time sleep as the previous day but woke only once in the night crying on and off for 50 minutes. On the third day I told the parents that they should not go in at all during the lunch-time nap. Her pattern was the same as the previous two days. However, in the night she had only one brief waking and settled herself back to sleep within 15 minutes. On the fourth day during her lunch-time nap she woke after 45 minutes and settled herself back to sleep within 15 minutes. She then woke again briefly after a further 45 minutes and settled herself back within five minutes. That night her parents heard her moaning and groaning when she came into her light sleep at 3am and again at 4.30am but she did not cry out.

For a further week during her lunch-time sleep she would cry out when she came into her light sleep but for shorter and shorter times. She continued to sleep well at night and by the end of two weeks she was back to her old routine of sleeping well at lunch-time, as well as at night. The crying and irritability in the late after-noon disappeared as she was no longer tired from lack of sleep. Harriet is now nearly two years old and continues to sleep well from 7pm–7.30am with a two-hour nap in the middle of the day.

Darkness and sleep

In the very early days babies are so transportable that many parents get into the habit of letting them fall asleep in the bouncy chair or car seat. This can be very convenient for the mother as it allows her to get out and about with the baby to do the shopping or visit friends. However, it does little to help establish regular nap times, which are conducive to a baby sleeping well at night.

The advice given by the majority of babycare experts on day-time sleep is that the baby should be put to sleep in a light room. This is supposed to help him distinguish between night and day and to sleep better at night. I totally disagree with this theory and believe it is the main cause of catnapping. In order to prevent a baby from developing the habit of catnapping, he must learn to have consolidated blocks of time asleep and time awake. I believe this can only be achieved if the baby learns the difference between awake time and asleep time in a dark, quiet room for sleep time and a bright, noisier room for awake time.

The following guidelines together with the routine appropriate to your baby's age will help you establish the proper quality day-time sleep for your baby, essential for long-term healthy sleep habits.

- During the early days of establishing day-time sleep, I believe it is essential that the morning and midday naps take place in the nursery in the dark with the door closed. Research has proved that the pineal gland produces a natural substance called mela-tonin, which works as a sedative. The release of this hormone is stimulated by darkness and prepares the body for sleep.
- All babies come into a light sleep after 45 minutes and even the smallest chink of light can be enough to prevent them from set-tling themselves back to sleep.
- A baby will only settle to sleep well if he is tired and ready to sleep. Babies under three months can normally stay awake for short spells between 1½ and 2 hours. Babies of three months and older can stay awake nearer two hours.

- Depending on the time of day, a baby will either have just been fed or fed two hours previously. In both instances the feed should be a full one. A baby who has not had a full feed will be harder to settle and, if he does sleep, the sleep rarely lasts as long as it should.
- If a baby settles easily without assistance at some of his sleep times but not others, hunger could be the cause. This often happens at the noon sleep or after 6.15pm. For several consecutive days the breast-fed baby should be offered a top-up of expressed milk and the formula-fed, an extra ounce or two at 11.45am and after the 6.15pm feed.

Joseph, aged ten weeks

Joseph was a fourth baby, and like his brother and two sisters, went straight into the routine. He was a very happy baby who fed and slept well. At six weeks he was sleeping through to 5am from his 11pm feed. Joseph's brother and sisters had all slept through the night from the time they were eight weeks. It therefore came as a bit of a shock to his mother when he reached ten weeks and was still waking at 5am. She would give him the benefit of the doubt that he might be hungry and offer him the breast. He would suck for a couple of minutes, then begin to scream hysterically and arch his back, refusing to feed. The mother, eventually realising he was not waking because of hunger, ended up cuddling him back to sleep. The procedure would take just over an hour with him falling asleep around 6.15am and waking of his own accord again at 7am. He would then happily take a full breast feed and follow the routine to the letter for the rest of the day. The mother could not fathom what was causing these early morning wakings. His day-time sleep was perfect. He fed well and his room had both a blackout blind and curtains lined with blackout material.

Obviously with three other children to take care of, starting the day at 5am began to take its toll on Joseph's mother. When she rang me for advice I could think of no obvious reason for the early morning waking. I suggested she should sleep with Joseph for a couple of nights to monitor his sleeping pattern.

She fed him his one formula feed of the day at 10.30pm and had him back in his cot and tucked in very securely by 11.30pm. She checked that the curtains were properly drawn and the door securely closed before settling herself down to sleep. At different intervals throughout the night he came into a light sleep, moving his body for a few minutes, sometimes groaning a little before going back to sleep. Then at 4.45am a bright stream of light appeared from under the bedroom door. Joseph immediately began to stir. He tossed his head from side to side and within ten minutes Joseph had pushed himself to the top of the cot. His head then turned to the direction of the stream of light under the door and he began to thrash his arms and legs up and down in the air and cry hysterically.

The cause of the problem became obvious. Slight subsidence in the family's very old house created a gap of nearly one inch under Joseph's bedroom door. Sudden light from the hallway when Joseph's father left for work in the City was enough to arouse him from light sleep. The Moro reflex was still strong enough to cause him to get into a hysterical state after he worked his way loose from the bedcovers.

I advised the parents to fit a draft excluder to the bottom of the door to block out the light and put Joseph in a lightweight sleeping bag at night. The sleeping bag, along with tucking in the sheet well around the cot would prevent him from moving up in the cot. Despite the above measures, I imagined Joseph would continue to wake at 5am out of habit, but because he had in the past refused to feed, I advised his mother not to rush to him when he stirred at 5am. The first three days he grizzled on and off for 30–40 minutes, then settled back to sleep until 7am. From then on Joseph has slept through until 7am every morning.

Each month I speak to dozens of parents who have similar problems. If your baby is under six months of age and waking early every morning not looking for a feed, it is important to check that he is not getting out of his blankets. For babies and toddlers of all ages, even the smallest chink of light can rouse them from their early morning light sleep or even their day-time nap.

Difficulties in settling

If your baby is difficult to settle at nap times it is essential that you pay particular attention to the time you begin settling him and how long you spend trying to do this. With the majority of babies, the main reason they are hard to settle is overtiredness or overstimulation. Once you are confident that you have your baby's feeding and sleeping on track, I would strongly advise you to help your baby learn how to settle himself to sleep. Although it will be very difficult to listen to him cry, he will very quickly learn how to go to sleep by himself. Refer to page 66 for details on crying down, a method that allows you to reassure your baby without assisting him to sleep. From my experience in helping hundreds of parents with babies who have had serious sleeping problems, once a baby learns how to settle himself, he becomes happier and more relaxed. Once proper day-time sleep is established, night-time sleep will also improve.

The following guidelines should help your baby learn how to settle himself.

- A baby who is allowed to fall asleep on the breast or bottle and is then put in the cot will be more likely to have disruptive nap times. When he comes into a light sleep 30–45 minutes after falling asleep, he will be less likely to settle himself back to sleep without your help. If your baby falls asleep while feeding, put him on the changing mat and rearrange his nappy. This should rouse him enough to go down in the cot semi-awake.
- Overtiredness is a major cause of babies not settling and not sleeping well during the day. A baby under three months who is allowed to stay awake longer than two hours at a time may get so overtired that he goes on to fight sleep for a further two hours. After three months the majority of babies, as they get older, will manage to stay awake slightly longer, sometimes up to 2½ hours at a time. A close eye should be kept on all babies after they have been awake for 1¾ hours so that you do not miss the cue for sleep.
- Overhandling prior to sleep time is another major problem with young babies. Everyone wants just one little cuddle. Unfortunately, several little cuddles add up and can leave the baby fretful, overtired and difficult to settle. Your baby is not a toy. Do not feel guilty about restricting the handling in the early weeks, especially prior to sleep time. Allow a wind down time of at least twenty minutes before nap time.
- Overstimulation prior to sleep time is another major cause of babies not settling well. Babies under six months should be allowed a quiet time of 20 minutes before being put down to sleep. With babies over six months, avoid games and activities that cause them to get overexcited. With all babies, regardless

of age, avoid excessive talking at put down time. Talk quietly and calmly using the same simple phrases: 'Night night, teddy. Night night, dolly. Sweet dreams.' Once you leave the room do not keep going back to check.

- The wrong sleep associations can also cause long-term sleep problems. It is essential that a baby goes down in his cot awake and learns to settle himself. For a baby who has already learned the wrong sleep associations, this problem can rarely be solved without some amount of crying. Fortunately, the majority of babies, if they are allowed, will learn to settle themselves within a few days. Refer to Chapter 3 for advice on crying down and controlled crying.

Excessive night waking

Until the mother's milk comes in, a newborn baby may wake and need to be fed several times a night. By the end of the first week, a baby who weighs over 7lb should manage to sleep for a stretch of four hours from the 10-11pm feed provided their feeding needs are being fully met during the day. Smaller babies may still need to feed three hourly around the clock. In my experience all babies who are healthy and well fed will, between four and six weeks of age, manage to sleep one longer spell of 5–6 hours. By following my routines in *The Contented Little Baby Book* this longer spell should happen in the night. The main aim of my routines is to help parents structure their baby's feeding and sleeping needs during the day so as to avoid excessive night waking.

How long a baby will continue to wake for a feed in the night depends very much on the individual baby. Some babies between six and eight weeks sleep through after the 10pm feed, others between ten and 12 weeks. Some may even take longer. All babies will sleep through the night as soon as they are physically and mentally able, provided the day-time feeding and sleeping is being properly structured. Listed below are the main causes of excessive night-time waking in healthy babies under one year old:

- Sleeping too much during the day. Even very small babies need to be awake some of the time. The baby should be encouraged to stay awake for 1–1½ hours after day-time feeds. Between six and eight weeks most babies are capable of staying awake for up to two hours.

- Not feeding enough during the day. If excessive night feeding is to be avoided the baby needs to have six feeds between 7am and 11pm . To fit in this number of feeds, the day must start at 7am.
- Not feeding enough at each feed. In the early days a baby needs a minimum of 25 minutes on one breast. A baby who weighs over 8lb should be offered the second breast.
- Breast-fed babies will be more likely to wake several times a night if they do not get enough to eat at the 10pm feed and may need a top-up after this feed.
- Babies under six weeks have a very strong Moro reflex and can wake themselves several times a night by the sudden startle and jerk. These babies will benefit from being swaddled in a lightweight stretch cotton sheet.
- Older babies often wake several times at night because they have kicked their covers off and are cold or they may have got their legs caught between the spars of the cot. A sleeping bag will help them avoid becoming cold and will prevent them from getting their legs caught in the spars.
- The baby has learned the wrong sleep associations. Between two and three months his sleep cycle changes and he will come into a light sleep several times at night. If the baby is used to being fed, rocked or given a dummy to get to sleep, he will need the same assistance to resettle himself in the night.
- Parents who leave the nursery door open or leave on a night light are more likely to be woken several times a night.
- If the baby's milk feeds are reduced too quickly when solids are introduced, he will begin to wake in the night genuinely needing a milk feed.

Early morning waking

All babies and young children come into a light sleep between 5 and 6am. Some will settle back to sleep for a further hour or so but many do not. I believe there are two things that determine whether a baby will become an earlier riser. One is the darkness of the nursery. It would be an understatement to say I am obsessed with how dark the nursery should be but I am totally convinced that it is the reason the majority of my babies quickly resettle themselves to sleep when they come into a light sleep at 5–6am. Once the nursery door is shut and the curtains drawn it should be so dark that not even the faintest trace of toys or books can be seen. Even a glimpse of these things will be enough to fully waken a baby from a drowsy state, wanting to start the day (see Joseph, page 41).

How parents deal with early wakings during the first three months will also determine whether their baby will become a child who is an early riser. During the first few weeks, a baby who is waking and feeding between 2 and 2.30am may wake around 6am and genuinely need to feed. However, it is essential to treat this feed like a night-time feed. It should be done as quickly and quietly as possible with the use of only a small socket night light and without talking or eye contact. The baby should then be settled back to sleep until 7–7.30am. If possible, avoid changing the nappy as this usually wakes up the baby too much.

Once the baby is sleeping and feeding nearer 4am, waking at 6am is not usually related to hunger. This is the one and only time I would advise parents to help their baby return to sleep. At this stage the most important thing is to get him back to sleep quickly, even if it means cuddling him and offering him a dummy until 7am. Listed below are guidelines that will help your baby not to become an early riser.

- Avoid using a night-light or leaving the door open. Research shows that chemicals in the brain work differently in the dark, preparing it for sleep. Even the smallest chink of light can be enough to awaken the baby fully when he enters his light sleep.
- Kicking off the bedcovers can also cause babies under six months to wake early. In my experience all babies under this age sleep better if tucked in securely. The sheet needs to be placed lengthways across the width of the cot to ensure that a minimum of 20cm (8ins) is tucked in at the far side and a minimum of 10cm (4ins) is tucked in at the near side. I would also advise rolling up a small hand towel and pushing it down between the spars and the mattress at the near side.
- Babies who work their way up the cot and get out of the covers will benefit from being put in a lightweight 100 per cent cotton sleeping bag and tucked in with a sheet as described above. Depending on the weather, blankets may not be necessary.
- Once a baby starts to move around the cot and is capable of rolling I would advise that you remove the sheets and blankets and use only the sleeping bag. This will allow your baby to move around unrestricted, without the worry that he might get cold in the middle of the night. It is important to choose a sleeping bag that is suitable for the time of year.

- Do not drop the 10pm feed until your baby has reached four months and has started solids. If he goes through a growth spurt before he starts solids, he can be offered extra milk at this time. This reduces the chances of waking early due to hunger, which can occur if the 10pm feed is dropped too soon.
- A baby who is over four months and has dropped the 10pm feed should be encouraged to stay awake until 7pm. If he is falling into a deep sleep before this time he will be much more likely to wake before 7am.

Sophia: aged four weeks

Sophia weighed nearly 10lb at birth and went straight into the two-to-four-week routine. She fed well and slept well at the right times. When she reached four weeks she started sleeping through till 6.30–7.30am from her 10pm feed. She had done this consistently for two weeks when suddenly she started waking at 5am.

Sophia's mother sent me her feeding and sleeping details for the last two weeks which showed that she was following the routine to the letter. She was feeding well and gaining 8oz each week. Baffled by the sudden backtrack on her night-time sleep, I decided to spend a day with the family. Throughout the whole day I saw no obvious reason for Sophia's early waking. At 10pm she was woken by the father for her formula feed. She drank very quickly and by 10.20pm there was only 1oz of feed left. Sophia started to get very sleepy and even the nappy change did not wake her up. She took the last ounce in a very drowsy state and was back in bed by 10.35pm.

I came to the conclusion that this very quick and rather sleepy feed was the cause of Sophia's early morning waking. Until a baby is between three and four months old, she will need to wake up properly somewhere between 7pm and 7am. Because Sophia had dropped her middle of the night feed and was very sleepy at the 10pm feed, her waking time had moved to 5am.

I suggested to the parents that for the following week they should wake Sophia as normal at 10pm but not feed her until 10.20pm. This would ensure that she was properly awake before she began feeding. They should only give her ⅔ of the feed before her nappy change. Then, instead of giving her the remainder straightaway, they should wait 15–20 minutes. During this time she could be laid on their bed for a stretch and a kick to make sure she was properly awake, but they were to avoid lots of talk and eye contact as this could confuse her, making her think it was day time. After 20 minutes they should dim the lights and offer her the remainder of her feed and settle her back in bed by 11.30pm at the latest. Within three nights Sophia was back to sleeping right through to 7am. I advised the parents to continue with this longer waking at 10pm for the rest of the week and then gradually to reduce the length of time she was awake by ten minutes. Provided she continued to sleep through to 7am, they should continue reducing the time awake by 10 minutes every three days. By the time she reached ten weeks, Sophia was able to sleep through to 7am with only a 30-minute waking at the 10pm feed.

Teething and night-time waking

In my experience, babies who enjoy a routine from a very early age and have established healthy sleeping habits are rarely bothered by teething. Out of the 300 babies I have helped care for, only a handful have been bothered by teething in the night. In these cases it is usually when the molars come through and then only for a few nights. I have found that babies who wake in the night due to teething are more likely to have suffered from colic and have developed poor sleeping habits.

If your baby is teething and waking in the night but quickly settles back to sleep when given a cuddle or a dummy, teething is probably not the real cause of his waking. A baby who is genuinely bothered by teething pain would be difficult to settle back to sleep. He would also shows signs of discomfort during the day, not just at night. I would advise you to check the section on excessive night waking (page 45) and early morning waking (page 46) to eliminate other reasons your baby may be waking. I often find at around six months of age many babies begin to kick their covers off, which can cause them to wake in the night. The majority of parents who contact me regarding their baby's teething and night waking report an immediate improvement when they follow my advice and put their baby in a sleeping bag at night.

If you are convinced that your baby's night-time wakings are caused by severe teething pain, I suggest you seek advice from your doctor regarding the use of paracetamol. While genuine teething pain may cause a few disruptive nights, it should never last for several weeks. If your baby seems out of sorts, develops a fever and suffers from loss of appetite or diarrhoea he should be seen by a doctor. Do not assume that these symptoms are just a sign of teething. Very often I have found that what parents thought was teething turned out to be an ear or throat infection.

Illness: the effect on sleep

The majority of my first babies manage to get through the first year without suffering the usual colds and coughs that seem to plague my second and third babies. By the time my first babies experience a cold their sleep is so well established that wakings in the night are very rare. With my second and third babies this is not the case as they usually catch their first cold at a much younger age from a brother or sister and disruptive nights are inevitable. A baby under three months of age will usually need help to get through the night when they have a cold or are ill. A young baby with a cold can get very distressed, especially when he is feeding, as he will not have learned to breathe through his mouth.

When a sick baby needs attention in the evening and during the night it should be given calmly and quietly. I believe that a sick baby needs more rest than a healthy baby. Lots of visitors and activity in the nursery during the evening and in the night should be avoided. When I have had to care for a sick baby who wakes several times at night I find it less disruptive to the routine if I sleep in the same room as the baby. It also enables me to attend to him quickly and I am less likely to disrupt the sleep of elder siblings by to-ing and fro-ing along the corridor.

Occasionally, I find that an older baby who has dropped night-time feeds will, once he has recovered, continue to wake up in the night looking for the same attention he received when he was unwell. For the first few nights I would check him and offer him some cool boiled water, but once I was convinced he was totally recovered, I would get tough and leave him to settle himself. In my experience, parents who are not prepared to do this usually end up with a baby who develops a long term sleep problem.

If your baby develops a cold or cough, regardless how mild it appears, he should be seen by a doctor. All too often I hear from distressed parents of babies with serious chest infections, which possibly could have been avoided if they had been seen by a doctor earlier. Too many mothers delay taking their baby to the doctor, worried that they will be classed as neurotic, but it is important that you discuss with your doctor any concerns you have about your baby's health, no matter how small. If your baby is ill it is essential that you follow to the letter your doctor's advice, especially on feeding.

Freddy and Isabella: aged five months

The twins were fed three-hourly when they were first born. By the end of the second week their feeding and weight gain were so good that they could go on the two-to-four-week routine. Both babies continued to feed well and adapted easily to the gradual changes in the routine. By 12 weeks both babies were sleeping through to 7am from their last feed at 10pm. They did this consistently until they were four months when they caught colds, which quickly developed into chest infections. Both babies began to wake several times a night because of difficulty in breathing. Their mother spent much of the night holding one baby or the other, as they only managed to sleep short spells before waking up, in a distressed state. Following advice by the doctor, they were offered fluids several times a night to avoid dehydration.

Unfortunately, once they were fully recovered both babies continued to wake up two or three times a night and would not settle back to sleep without a cuddle and a drink. This pattern went on for nearly three weeks until sleep deprivation began to have a serious effect on the twins and their mother. She became physically and mentally exhausted from getting up several times a night and coping with two very tired, irritable babies during the day. The doctor advised her to try and break the habit of their waking at night by using the controlled crying method (see page 67). The mother attempted this for two nights but found the five hours of continuous crying between both babies too hard to bear.

It was at this stage she rang me in the hope that I knew another method that would break the habit of excessive night-time wakings. I explained that the controlled crying method was the most effective way to treat this very common problem, but I suggested altering the approach slightly. When dealing with two babies who are waking more than once at night, I find it better to eliminate the wakings one at a time.

The babies' waking times were fairly consistent: around 1am, 3am and 5am. I suggested that she eliminate the waking at 1am first. This would be quite easy, as the babies were still having a small feed at 10pm. I advised her, on the first night, to wait until 11.45pm before feeding the babies. They both took nearly 150ml (5oz) at this time and settled back to sleep quickly. They slept through the usual 1am waking time and woke at 2.15am. As planned, their mother checked them every 10–15 minutes but did not pick up or speak to either of them. Both babies then cried on and off for over an hour before waking again around 5am. This time the mother went straight to them and settled them back to sleep with a drink of well-diluted juice and a cuddle. They then slept until 7am.

The second night they both woke at 2.45am. Their mother followed the same plan as the first night, only this time she extended the interval of going in to every 20 minutes. They both cried on and off for just under one hour, settling back to sleep by 3.40am. They then woke around 6.30am but she waited until 7am before feeding them.

On the third night we agreed that she should wait 30 minutes before going in to check them. Both babies slept through to 3.25am. Freddy cried for ten minutes and settled himself back to sleep and Isabella cried for 35 minutes before settling herself back to sleep. Because Isabella's cry was calming down after 25 minutes, her mother decided not to go in to her. They both awoke around 6.50am.

The fourth night Freddy slept through to 7am and Isabella to 5am. She cried on and off for 40 minutes before settling herself back to sleep. Like the previous night Isabella's crying was very on and off so the mother decided not to go in.

On the fifth night there was a lot of loud groaning between 5.30am and 6am but neither baby cried out and both had to be woken at 7am. They were fed at 11.45pm for a further two nights. As both babies continued to sleep through to 7am, I suggested this feed should be brought forward by ten minutes every couple of nights until they were back to feeding at 10pm.

I then advised the mother to reduce the amount they were fed at 10pm by 30ml (1oz) and if they continued to sleep through, to continue reducing it by a further 30ml (1oz) every three nights. Within nine days the 10pm feed was reduced to 60ml (2oz). As both babies were still sleeping through to 7am, I advised the mother to drop the feed altogether. The babies are nearly 20 months old now and both have continued to sleep well from 7pm–7am every morning.

3
Crying in the first year

In the very early days, crying is the only way a baby has of communicating his needs to his parents. How often and how long a baby cries will depend on the parent's ability to understand his needs and the cause of his crying.

Many parents, especially first time parents, have great difficulty in trying to fathom why their baby is crying. It can be very distressing for both parents and baby if the baby refuses to be calmed, despite checking the obvious list of feeding, burping, changing, cuddling, etc.

In my first book I stress the importance of establishing regular feeding and sleeping times from the very beginning. I am convinced it is because my routines are structured to meet all my babies' basic needs that crying is kept to a minimum – and they certainly rarely cry from hunger or overtiredness.

Dr C R Jayachandra, a former consultant paediatrician at the Royal Oldham Hospital and author of the book *Screaming Babies*, also believes in the importance of routine. He maintains that persistent crying in a healthy baby is not only curable but preventable. He advises that a baby should be offered regular feeds, allowed to control intake and not handled when he wants to be left alone. He used to teach child management techniques to parents who have screaming babies and it is his belief that it is parents' mismanagement of the baby's needs that causes stress for the baby and makes a baby cry excessively.

Crying: normal or excessive

As I mentioned earlier, crying is the only means a young baby has of communicating his needs to his parents. How they interpret and respond to it will determine how long the crying continues. A baby whose basic needs are met will be happy and content, but it is normal for even the happiest and most contented baby to cry at times.

Research done by the Thomas Coram Research Unit at London University says that most young babies cry on average for a total of two hours a day. Dr St James-Roberts claims that crying reaches a peak at around six weeks of age, with 25 per cent of babies crying and fussing up to four hours a day. He also says 40 per cent of this crying occurs between 6pm and midnight.

Dutch researchers Van de Rijt and Plooij have spent over twenty years studying baby development and have written a book called *Why They Cry*. They believe babies cry more when going through one of the major neurological changes that occur during the first year. These changes usually come at five, eight, 12, 15, 23, 34 and 42 weeks of age. Certainly I have noticed that my babies do become more fussy and unsettled at certain times and these tend to coincide with growth spurts. However, as discussed in my first book, I would be absolutely horrified if any of my babies cried for even one hour a day, let alone two to four!

Some of my babies will fuss and fret when being undressed. Others scream when their nappy is changed and some, regardless how much they are cuddled at bedtime, will need a short yell before going off to sleep. Nearly all babies will have an unsettled period in the late afternoon and may need extra attention to get through it. At the end of any given day, if I were to add up the total amount of crying, it would rarely amount to more than 15–20 minutes – nothing like the 2–4 hours baby experts consider normal. The only time I have to deal with excessive crying is when I am called in to help parents who are at the end of their tether trying to cope with an unhappy, screaming baby. These babies are always feeding on demand and without structured sleep times. From my experience, lack of routine is a major factor in causing these babies to cry so much. I have never seen excessive crying in any of the babies I have put into a routine from the very early days.

The following extracts taken from some of the many letters I have received from parents using my first book also confirm how my routines have helped reduce their babies' excessive crying.

Reader from London: 'Nothing short of miraculous'

'As a second-time mum, I thought I knew how to cope. I hadn't bargained for my little bundle of fury. Feeding every two hours night and day, screaming for most of the rest of the time, my daughter was tense, unhappy and difficult. A neighbour took pity on me one morning and lent me this book, which transformed our family's life in 24 hours. Gina explains why her methods work and her calm, knowing approach gives a desperate parent the confidence to follow the advice. Once you see what it is your baby actually needs (as opposed to what you think she needs) any doubts you may have had about the regime vanish. I can't recommend it highly enough.'

Reader from Birmingham: 'Buy this book'

'Gina's book is an excellent guide for confused, first-time parents, overawed by the responsibility of a new life entrusted to them to nurture. Her routines seem to really suit our son Sam, who is a very contented little baby – corny but true. The routine also helped us to learn his different cries and to distinguish between happy / bored / lonely / tired / put me down / feed me / pick me up, etc. He is no longer colicky, sleeps when he teethes and when he is sick – which is what he needs to get well. Gina has really helped us to enjoy each other to the full with confidence, energy and enthusiasm.'

Reader from Cambridge: 'No question, this book is excellent. A must for parents.'

'Before we followed this book, our baby was overtired, crying six hours a day and awake 2–4 times a night, probably had colic and we were all miserable. Now the joy of parenthood has returned, smiles, laughs, etc. She now cries less than one hour a day and wakes once at night! Our baby girl is breast fed, seven weeks old and we have followed Gina Ford for two weeks. Our daughter followed the Gina routine from the first day. The change was instantaneous and she continues to go from strength to strength.'

Following the routines in my first book will go a long way towards ensuring that your baby's basic needs are met. They will also help avoid much of the excessive crying in the early days, which experts claim is normal. Here are other reasons for crying.

Hunger in the early days

During the first week of life hunger is the most common reason for babies to cry. At this stage it is best to assume that any crying is due to hunger and therefore the baby should always be offered a feed. However, once the milk comes in, some sort of pattern should emerge. A breast-fed baby who has had a good feed should be happy to go for a stretch of three hours from the beginning of his last feed. Some babies would, if allowed, actually go longer but I would advise against this in the early days. Until a baby has regained his birth weight, I believe it is better to wake him for a feed every three hours. Regular feeding will also help establish a good milk supply from the outset and reduce the likelihood of a baby crying due to hunger. A well-fed baby should regain his birth weight between ten and fourteen days and continue to have a weight gain of 6–8oz each week. If your baby is over two weeks old and not gaining this amount of weight, it is very possible that excessive crying is due to hunger. Low milk supply during the third week is a common problem with breast-fed babies. I would advise that you read page 3 carefully on how to increase the milk supply. With a formula-fed baby it is usually easier to tell if hunger is the problem by the amount he is drinking. The amount a formula-fed baby needs is determined by his weight. Check page 9 for guidelines on the number of feeds needed in 24 hours and the individual amount to be given at each feed.

Hunger and the older baby

Between four and five months the majority of babies show signs of needing more than just milk to satisfy their hunger. Careful attention should be given to the introduction of solids to ensure that a baby receives the right balance of milk and solids to satisfy his hunger. Babies still being milk fed in the middle of the night will be less likely to take to solids. This can lead to excessive milk feeding and the baby becoming a 'milkoholic', refusing all other food. As milk alone no longer meets the nutritional needs of a baby approaching six months of age, he soon becomes hungry and irritable. To avoid this happening it is important that once solids are established, any middle of the night feeds are dropped. It is also important that the 10pm feed should be gradually reduced and eventually dropped as the baby increases his solids. While milk is still an important part of the baby's diet, it is essential that by six months of age the number of milk feeds are reduced to four, encouraging the baby to increase his intake of solids.

Thomas: aged six months

Thomas weighed nearly 10lb at birth and was breast fed on demand for the first three months. At four months he weighed nearly 17lb and was weaned onto formula. He was drinking approximately 210ml (7oz) of formula every 3–3½ hours, well in excess of 1440ml (48oz) each day. At least two of these feeds were in the middle of the night. His mother, exhausted from getting up twice in the night to feed Thomas and concerned about his excessive milk intake, approached her health visitor for advice. The health visitor advised her to introduce solids at four months and reassured her that Thomas's milk feed would reduce once solids were established. She started Thomas on a small amount of baby rice after the 2pm feed. He only took a couple of mouthfuls and started to scream. He responded the same way the following day and, in desperation to get him to take the rice, she mixed it with half a jar of fruit purée. Although he still protested, he did take a few teaspoonfuls. Over the weeks that followed, Thomas was offered a variety of fruit and vegetables. His response was always the same. He would take a few teaspoonfuls, then start to cry.

By five months Thomas was still waking and feeding in the night but now he was more difficult to settle back to sleep, often crying on and off until the next feed. Because the crying was accompanied by much hand chewing his mother assumed that he was teething. At six months the crying and constant hand chewing were such a problem that she rang me for advice. I suggested during the following two days that she write down complete details of Thomas's feeding, sleeping and crying. When I received his details it was immediately clear to me that the cause of excessive crying and hand chewing was hunger, not teething.

Thomas now weighed over 19lb and was only eating two or three teaspoonfuls of fruit at breakfast, a couple of cubes of veg-

etables at lunch-time and four teaspoonfuls of baby rice in the evening. Because he was still feeding twice in the night, his daily intake of milk was so excessive that he was not increasing his solids during the day. Although the amount of food required varies from baby to baby, the quantity of solids Thomas was consuming was very low for his size.

To increase the amount of solids he was eating, his mother would have to reduce his milk intake very quickly. I suggested that for the next two days she eliminate the 2pm milk feed and replace it with well-diluted juice. This would cause Thomas to be hungrier at 5pm and eat more solids. The increase in solids would help reduce his middle of the night milk feeds. We also agreed that Thomas should only be fed once in the night. At all other wakings he should be offered water or well-diluted juice.

The first evening he took an extra teaspoonful of baby rice and slept past his usual 11pm waking, sleeping until 1.30am. His mother then offered him some cool boiled water, which he absolutely refused. She then offered some very well diluted juice, which he drank before settling back until 5am. As he had already dropped two feeds that night, she offered him a full 240ml (8oz) milk feed. He then settled back until 7am.

The second day he increased his lunch-time solids to three cubes of vegetables and in the evening took 5½ teaspoonfuls of baby rice. That night he slept through until 3am and settled back to sleep until 7am after being offered a drink of well-diluted juice. Because he had cut out three night feeds in two days, I advised his mother to reintroduce a very small milk feed at 2pm to ensure his daily milk intake was a minimum 600ml (20oz), as recommended by health authorities.

Over the next four nights Thomas would wake once somewhere between 3 and 5am, drink his well-diluted juice and settle back to sleep until 7am. By the seventh day Thomas was eating a small amount of breakfast cereal after his morning formula feed and having four cubes of vegetable and chicken casserole at lunch-time with his formula feed. He then had a small formula feed at 2pm and in the evening he was having six teaspoons of baby rice and two cubes of fruit purée after his formula feed.

That night he slept right through from 7pm–7am. I advised his mother that it was very important to continue gradually decreasing his lunch-time milk feed and to increase his solids in order to meet his growing appetite and nutrition requirements. When he was down to only 90ml (3oz) of formula and his solids increased to 6–7 cubes of chicken and vegetable casserole, the lunch-time milk feed should be dropped. He should then be offered a drink of water or well-diluted juice from a beaker. In the evening his baby rice should be gradually increased to eight teaspoonfuls mixed with some formula milk and a small amount of fruit purée.

By the time Thomas reached seven months he was enjoying three well-balanced meals a day plus the correct amount of milk recommended for his age. He continued to sleep well at night and all the crying and hand chewing had disappeared.

Thirst

According to the majority of childcare experts it is not essential to give a young baby water, especially breast-fed babies. However, once the milk supply is established I personally believe that a couple of ounces of water do no harm and will often calm a fractious baby, especially in hot weather.

- Breast-fed babies should be offered water no more than once a day and midway between feeds. Avoid giving water one hour before the feed because it can reduce the baby's appetite.
- Formula-fed babies can get thirstier than breast-fed babies and if necessary can be offered water a couple of times a day midway between feeds.
- Water should always be boiled and allowed to cool before being offered to a baby. Tap water should ideally be filtered before boiling to remove toxic chemicals and inorganic residue. If bottled water is used it must be a low sodium brand such as Evian or Highland Spring.
- A breast-fed baby under four months who is drinking more than a couple of ounces of water at any one time but is gaining less than 180ml (6oz) of weight per week is possibly being underfed. Refer to advice on page 3 to increase milk supply.

Wind and breast-fed babies

Breast-fed babies will not always bring up wind after a feed. As long as they are happy it is best not to spend ages trying to wind them. The endless rubbing and patting on the back can actually cause more upset than the wind itself. Breast-fed babies who are positioned incorrectly on the breast are more likely to be bothered by wind. Frequently I observe mothers holding their babies as if they were bottle feeding. This means the baby is not able to latch onto the breast properly and results in his taking in more air than necessary. If you are confident you have the positioning correct, it is possible that the wind may be caused by something you are eating. Occasionally I have noticed that some babies react badly after the mother has eaten certain foods. For more advice on healthy eating and producing good quality breast milk, refer to page 22.

Wind and bottle-fed babies

Bottle-fed babies tend to take in more wind than breast-fed babies but this should not create a problem if the baby is given the opportunity to burp once during the feed and once at the end. It is often assumed that burping a bottle-fed baby after every ounce will result in the baby taking in less wind. I frequently find the baby's crying is more likely to be caused by the distress of the bottle constantly being removed from his mouth than by the wind itself. If your bottle-fed baby has problems bringing up his wind, which leaves him in lots of discomfort, refer to page 22 for more details of formula feeding and the causes of wind.

Colic

Excessive crying in babies under three months is more often than not diagnosed as colic. The 'colicky baby' is usually described as being in great pain, screaming as he brings his knees up to his tummy, which is often distended and noisy. These long crying spells usually start in late afternoon or early evening and can last for several hours at a time. Opinion among healthcare experts is divided about what colic really is and some do not believe it even exists. Others believe that an immature digestive system and intestinal pain may be the causes of the crying and distended tummy.

Penelope Leach, author of several bestselling books on parenting and childcare, says in her book *Baby and Child* that colic is not an illness that needs diagnosis and treatment. She describes colic as a very distressing pattern of new-born behaviour with no known cause, no treatment and absolutely no ill effects except on parents' nerves. She believes parents should accept that the cause of colic is unknown and there is very little they can do. She advises parents not to search continually for a cause as it will only confuse other aspects of babycare by changing feeds, feeding techniques and routines, all to no avail. She suggests parents should instead concentrate on organising their life so that they have enough energy to give the baby the attention he needs during a 'colicky time'.

Dr Miriam Stoppard says in her *Baby Care Book* that a baby is very quick to pick up tension. She believes that the excessive crying may be a response to the mother's evening hypersensitiveness. Parents are advised never to leave their baby to cry. They should try to soothe their baby by rocking him or taking him for a ride in the car or in a pram, even at night. For a mother on her own, she advises putting the baby in a sling and just letting him cry while she gets on with whatever it is she needs to do. She also suggests trying to relax the baby with various sounds such as singing, calm music, the television or vacuum cleaner.

Dr Richard Ferber, in his book *Solve Your Child's Sleep Problems*, takes the view that a colicky baby is either oversensitive to things going on around him or is exposed to excessive amounts of handling and other stimulation. He believes that this 'chaotic' input is difficult for the baby to handle and may stem from a buildup of tension throughout the day to the point where his coping abilities become overloaded. Ferber disagrees with the majority of other experts' advice about how to deal with colic. He says if the baby's needs were to be held, fed or rocked, or just suck on a pacifier, these interventions would calm him. He advises that these babies should be given the opportunity to discharge tension at the end of the day. His guidelines are:

- If the baby cannot be easily comforted, allow him to cry alone for 15–30 minutes.
- If he has not settled by then, you may try to console or feed him once again in a very calm, soft-spoken and gentle manner.
- Parents should avoid trying to quieten the baby by bouncing or similar vigorous stimulation. If gentle attempts are still not helpful they should allow the baby to cry for another 15- or 30-minute period.

Ferber believes that allowing the baby to cry undisturbed for two or three consecutive colicky periods will give him the chance to release the built-up tension. He claims that the baby will then be better able to 'organise' himself and feel comfortable with daily routines. Within one or two days, he says, the intensity of crying should decrease and the baby should sleep better.

Dr Brian Symon believes colic exists but he maintains it is a diagnosis that is overused and applied incorrectly. In his own practice it is his last choice as a diagnosis for excessive crying. In his book *Silent Nights* he says that for many parents colic simply means the baby is crying. He believes the most common causes of babies crying are hunger and overtiredness. His advice for dealing with colic is to ensure the baby is well fed, clean and dry, firmly wrapped but not over-wrapped or hot. The treatment is then the same as for overtired babies. Refer to page 66 for his method of crying down.

The cure

Experts are divided as to what causes colic but the majority agree that there is no magic cure. Both Leach and Stoppard take the view that colic is something that parents have to learn to live with and that it normally disappears within three months. Sadly for parents struggling to cope with a colicky baby, what should be the happiest time of their lives can turn out to be one of the most miserable. No amount of feeding, rocking, cuddling and walking will stop the hard and excessive crying. For the majority of parents the advice given by Ferber and Symon to put a baby in his cot and leave him to cry for 15-minute spells is unthinkable, probably because they have read the views of experts like Stoppard: a baby left to cry may develop long-term psychological problems.

Unfortunately, as many parents of a colicky baby can confirm, the colic does disappear at three months but the sleeping problems do not. All the rocking, cuddling, etc involved in trying to calm the baby usually lead to the wrong sleep associations. He still refuses to settle in the evening and often wakes several times in the night. Each time he wakes he expects to be fed, rocked or cuddled back to sleep. This problem can continue for many months and often years.

I am often asked how I coped when one of my babies suffered from colic. The honest answer is that not one of the hundreds of babies I have helped care for has ever suffered from colic. I am convinced this is because I structure their feeding and sleeping from day one.

Since publication of my first book, hundreds of parents have contacted me for advice about how to deal with their colicky baby. My advice is always the same: follow the routine to the letter. Those that do find their baby's colic usually disappears overnight!

I believe there are many different reasons for excessive evening crying, or colic. If your baby is crying for hours every evening, it could be for one of the many reasons listed below. By eliminating all these possible causes and following the routine appropriate for your baby's age in *The Contented Little Baby Book*, you should find your baby's excessive crying is greatly reduced.

- Many breast-fed babies are very unsettled in the evening because their mother's milk supply is low. Follow the advice on page 3 for increasing low milk supply and top up your baby with either a bottle of expressed or formula milk.
- Both breast-fed and bottle-fed babies should be fed no later than 2.15pm to ensure that they take a really good feed at 6.15pm.
- Babies being fed on demand are more prone to colic. Gradually increase the time between feeds until your baby is feeding at the times recommended in the routine, appropriate for his age.
- Babies who are allowed to sleep late in the morning are unlikely to settle at 7pm. Regardless of how your baby has slept at night, wake him at 7am. This will ensure that you can fit in the correct number of feeds before 7pm and that he has been awake enough time. Refer to page 38 for guidelines on the amount of day-time sleep your baby needs.
- Overstimulation prior to bedtime can result in a baby becoming overtired. Prior to the bath, start to wind things down – no loud noises or exciting games. Until the baby is settled in the routine, it is better if one person does the bath, feeding and settling. Constant handling from one person to another will only make a fretful baby worse.
- Overtiredness is one of the main reasons that so many babies do not settle in the evening. Babies who are used to catnapping on and off all day are more prone to overtiredness. Once you are confident that you are getting his feeding and sleeping right you may have to follow the advice for overtiredness on page 64. This advice will work provided you are sure your baby is getting enough milk to drink at the 6.15pm feed.

- A baby who is screaming at every feed and arching his back midway through a feed could be suffering from reflux and it would be worthwhile seeking medical advice.

Tiredness

With some babies it is obvious when they are getting tired. They will simply start to yawn and look sleepy. But with other babies it is not so easy to tell. The onset of tiredness often causes much crying, usually accompanied by arching of the back or bringing up of the legs. Unfortunately, many parents mistake a tired cry for hunger or colic. If a baby under six months of age displays these signs after 1½ to 2 hours of being awake, the cause is probably tiredness. Between six months and one year they can usually stay awake slightly longer but would certainly be getting tired after 2½ hours. In my first book I stress the importance of watching for any signals that indicate the baby is getting tired and with many babies it is crying.

Even if your baby does not show any signs of tiredness I would advise that you allow a 20-minute wind-down period prior to his sleep time. Take him to his room, dim the lights and give him a cuddle to get him really relaxed. Avoid lots of talking and eye contact. Once he is relaxed and looking sleepy put him in the cot and leave the room. Allow between 10 and 20 minutes for him to get himself to sleep. Do not be tempted to keep picking him up as constant handling will only result in his becoming so overtired that he fights sleep. A baby who is regularly allowed to become overtired will eventually only fall asleep through sheer exhaustion. This is rarely a deep relaxed sleep and can lead to long-term sleep problems.

Overtiredness

Overtiredness is a major cause of crying, and learning your baby's cue for tiredness can go a long way towards avoiding excessive crying at sleep times. The length of time a baby can stay awake before tiredness sets in varies from baby to baby. When babies are allowed to stay awake too long they usually become so overtired that they fight sleep. When they eventually fall asleep through exhaustion it is usually very restless and disturbed sleep and often lasts for only a very short time.

Babies who are regularly allowed to get overtired often need much patting and rocking to get to sleep and they usually end up catnapping all day. They very rarely achieve a regular pattern of deep refreshing sleep, which can leave them irritable and unhappy.

My routines in *The Contented Little Baby Book* give clear advice on the sleeping needs of babies during the first year. If followed to the letter, overtiredness is rarely a problem.

Kate: aged 5½ months

Kate had been happily following the routines since she was four weeks old. She had slept through the night from seven weeks and dropped her 10pm feed at four months. She settled easily at 7pm and had to be woken at 7am every morning. She also slept well between 9am and 9.45am and 12.15pm to 2.15pm as well as having a short catnap of ten minutes in her buggy in the late after-noon. When Kate reached five months, she suddenly started to cut back on her lunch-time nap. She would wake around 1.15pm and not settle back to sleep. At this stage her mother was not too con-cerned, since Kate got through the afternoon happily. She just assumed Kate was beginning to need less sleep.

One evening when Kate was around 5½ months, she refused to settle at 7pm. She screamed and screamed and could not be consoled. It was nearly 8.15pm before her mother managed to settle her. After four nights things were getting worse. Kate was screaming more and more and taking even longer to settle. Her mother began to panic. She was unused to Kate crying, certainly never for over an hour at a time.

She rang me on the fifth day, desperate for advice about how she could get Kate's bedtime back to being calm and happy. Since Kate's excessive crying at bedtime started suddenly at the same time as she cut back her lunch-time nap, I suspected the cause was overtired-ness. I suggested Kate's morning nap be cut back to 30 minutes to see if this would improve her lunch-time sleep. If this did not work and Kate still woke at 1.15pm, she should be encouraged to have a slightly longer nap at 4.30pm. Unfortunately, neither of these sug-gestions worked. Kate continued to get overtired at bedtime, crying excessively for more than an hour before going to sleep.

Although we could not solve the overtiredness problem by restructuring her sleep, I felt sure that we could reduce the exces-sive crying, which resulted from overtiredness.

I advised that once Kate was put in her cot to sleep she should be left, no matter how hard she cried. An overtired baby can rarely be calmed and to keep picking her up would only delay the length of time she took to go to sleep. (See below for details on crying down.) Unlike a baby who has a sleep association problem and may cry for hours, the overtired baby will, if allowed, usually fall asleep within 20 minutes.

I also suggested that Kate's bath and bedtime routine be brought forward by ten minutes so she did not become overtired and fractious when feeding.

The mother followed my advice and on the nights Kate was overtired she would cry for 10–20 minutes before going off to sleep. Although it was hard listening to her cry, Kate's mother agreed it was preferable to the hysterical state Kate got into when she tried to help her get to sleep.

When Kate reached seven months and started moving around more, regularly attending a swimming class and baby exercise class, she went back to sleeping longer at her lunch-time nap.

Crying down

Crying down is a term that has become fashionable over the last few years, particularly with sleep experts. Dr Brian Symon uses it to describe the pattern of crying when an overtired baby is going to sleep. Crying down, he says, is the reverse of crying up, crying up being the description of a baby waking up from a good sleep and starting to demand a feed. Crying up starts with silence. The baby is asleep. He wakes. His first sounds are soft, gentle, subtle. After a minute or two of being ignored the baby begins to cry. He will cry for a short spell, then go quiet for a short spell. If he is ignored the crying starts again but louder. Crying gradually increases in volume with the gaps between cries becoming shorter until the baby is emitting a continuous loud bellow.

Crying down, he explains, is the reverse of that picture. The overtired baby will start to bellow loudly when put down to sleep and the reverse pattern begins. The process of crying down can take between ten minutes and 30 minutes. The more overtired the baby is, the louder and longer he will cry. Dr Symon stresses that this technique will only work if the baby is allowed to settle himself to sleep. Parents who find the crying difficult to ignore are advised to wait ten minutes before going in. They can then enter and reassure the baby with a soothing touch or quiet voice. Reassurance must be kept to a maximum of one or two minutes. Parents should then wait a further 10–15 minutes before returning. For this technique to work it is essential that the baby is not picked up and the baby must be allowed to settle by himself in the cot.

Dr Symon believes that parents who do not allow their overtired baby to get himself off to sleep are creating long-term sleep problems. His beliefs have recently been confirmed by research at Oxford University. They conclude that a 20 minute 'winding down' bedtime routine, coupled with ignoring crying for gradually increasing intervals, is an effective way of dealing with babies and children who resist sleep.

Provided a baby has been well fed and is ready to sleep, I believe he should be allowed to settle himself. The above method works not only for overtired babies but also for babies who fight sleep. Although it is very difficult to listen to a young baby cry himself to sleep, it will prevent serious sleep problems in the future. Parents who are not prepared to leave their baby to cry for 10–20 minutes usually end up resorting to feeding, rocking or giving a dummy to induce sleep.

Filmed research shows that all babies come into a light sleep several times a night. Some will even wake up briefly before drifting back to sleep. Babies unable to drift back to sleep unaided are used to being rocked, given a dummy or fed to sleep. These babies will continue to wake up several times a night needing assistance to get back to sleep. As the months go by both parents and baby become exhausted and irritable from lack of sleep. In desperation to establish a healthy sleep pattern for their baby, some parents resort to a method called controlled crying. This method of sleep training does work provided parents can cope with hours of crying. These drastic measures could easily be avoided if parents allowed their young babies to settle themselves in the beginning.

Controlled crying

A baby who is in the habit of waking several times a night and needs assistance to get back to sleep is unlikely to develop long term healthy sleep habits. The fact that in the UK we have over 126 sleep clinics advising parents on babies' and children's sleeping problems would confirm this. Since publication of my first book, the majority of mothers who contact me for advice are those with older babies and toddlers. Most are waking several times a night and many have never slept through the night. All these babies and children have learned the wrong sleep associations, which is the cause of the many night wakings. Sadly there is no magical cure for this problem and most parents have to resort to controlled crying.

One of the most successful methods of sleep training has been devised by senior paediatrician, Dr Richard Ferber. Dr Ferber is widely recognised as America's leading authority in the field of children's sleep problems. His book *Solve Your Child's Sleep Problems* is a bestseller not only in America but in Great Britain. It explains every aspect of children's sleep in great detail, how problems evolve and how parents can resolve them. For older babies and children who are still feeding in the night he advises gradually eliminating night feeds. If waking continues he recommends controlled crying to break the habit. The controlled crying method is likely to be more successful if used at each of the baby's sleep times. While this method does teach a baby or child how to get to sleep on his own, it can be difficult to endure and can fail because parents get very distressed listening to their baby or child cry for lengthy periods of time. They resort to picking up the baby after 30 or 40 minutes and rocking him to sleep, which usually creates an even worse sleep problem. The baby soon learns that if he cries long enough and hard enough, he will be picked up.

For sleep training to be successful it is essential that the baby or child learn to settle himself to sleep, no matter how long it takes. Sleep training can be both mentally and emotionally draining for parents and is not something that should be approached without considerable thought. If you decide to attempt it, it is essential that your baby or child has a medical check up and your doctor will then be able to confirm whether they are healthy enough to be sleep trained. It is also worthwhile seeking advice and support from your health visitor who will be able to put you in touch with your nearest sleep clinic.

The basic rules for controlled crying are as follows:

- Decide on a regular time to start the bedtime routine and stick to it. Allow at least one hour for the bath and settling.
- Settle your baby or child in his bed before he gets too sleepy. Kiss him goodnight and leave the room.
- Allow a minimum of 5–10 minutes of crying before returning to reassure him.
- Reassurance should be kept to a minimum and he must not be

picked up. Leave the room after a few minutes even if he continues to cry.

- The time between visits should be increased by 5–10 minutes each time. Reassurance should be kept to a maximum of a few minutes and the baby or child should never be lifted out of the cot.

Jack: aged five months

Jack's parents had read the book Three in a Bed and followed the advice of the author Deborah Jackson. Jack had slept in his parents' bed since birth and was breast fed on demand. However, contrary to claims by the author, co-sleeping and demand feeding did not result in a more secure, happy and contented baby. By the time Jack reached five months both parents were at their wits' end trying to cope with a baby who was still waking and feeding several times a night and was fussy and fretful all day. By evening, both parents were totally exhausted from trying to meet Jack's demands and they began to neglect the needs of his elder sister. Things eventually came to a head when the parents noticed a distinct change in their daughter's behaviour. Realising that sleep deprivation was beginning to affect every aspect of their family life, they contacted me for advice on how to get Jack to sleep by himself in a cot.

I suggested that they start by establishing a regular day-time and bedtime routine for Jack, settling him in his cot each sleep time. Once Jack was settled in his cot they were to use the controlled crying method to train him to sleep there.

The first evening he cried for 20 minutes at 7pm, then fell asleep. His mother woke him at 11pm for a quick feed and resettled him to sleep with a dummy. He woke at 2am when his mother tried to settle him back to sleep with a dummy. She continued to put it in his mouth every time he cried until eventually he fell asleep at 5am. His mother had to wake him at 7am and, for the first time ever, he emptied both breasts. I suggested the parents try to settle Jack without the dummy since using it to get him to sleep would only create a further problem. They were also to continue extending the length of time between checks.

On the second day Jack was settled in his cot for all his naps without the dummy. He would cry for 5–15 minutes before going off to sleep. That evening he fell asleep after 20 minutes of crying and had to be woken at 11pm for his feed. He settled quickly after that feed, slept until 4am and cried on and off until 5am before going back to sleep till 6.30am.

By the end of the first week Jack's sleeping pattern was still quite erratic. However, he was settling well at 7pm with very little crying, only waking once or twice in the night. He usually managed to settle himself back to sleep within 10–20 minutes and his parents no longer needed to use the checking method. By the end of the second week he was only waking once in the night, settling himself back to sleep within 5–10 minutes.

Jack was still being woken at 11pm to be fed and had begun cutting back on his morning feed so I suggested not waking him for an 11pm feed. For the next two nights he woke briefly at 1am but settled back within ten minutes, sleeping through until 6.30am.

Although it took 16 difficult and heart wrenching days and nights of controlled crying to train Jack to sleep through the night, his parents believe it was worth it. He is much happier, more contented and relaxed now, as are his parents and sister who are also getting a good night's sleep.

Boredom

During the first couple of weeks most of a baby's awake time is spent feeding, changing and burping. By the third week the majority of babies are beginning to get more alert and can stay awake longer. It is often around this age that parents say their baby becomes more unsettled. Next to getting feeding and sleeping right, it is important that the baby's mental and social needs are met. I believe even very young babies benefit greatly from visual stimulation and social activities. I have helped care for numerous sets of twins and premature babies and despite being so small, they were all introduced to colourful books and had certain toys to look at from the very beginning. They have all showed varying degrees of interest.

When playing with your baby, remember that he has a short concentration span so try not to overstimulate him. It is also important to encourage your baby to entertain himself for short spells. By six to eight weeks most babies will be happy to entertain themselves under their mobile or on the play mat for 15–20 minutes at a time. He will be more likely to do this if he is well fed and not overtired – and you are within eyesight.

Listed below are some of the most popular toys for babies under six months:

- A musical cot mobile will give hours of amusement to a young baby. It will also help develop his eye muscles as he follows the moving objects. Choose one that is brightly coloured and interesting to look at from underneath. Faces of animals and clowns are always great favourites. Remember to remove the mobile from the cot when your baby goes to sleep.

- A baby gym is a frame with a variety of toys hanging from it under which the baby lies. Some are attached to an activity mat and can be folded up when not in use. They come in an assortment of styles and colours but the black, red and white version is the one that seems to captivate babies' attention the most. A baby gym will encourage your baby to kick and develop his hand-eye coordination as he tries to grab the dangling toys. A very small baby may be more comfortable if a travel rug is placed on the floor under the baby gym.

- Black and white cot cloth books are always very popular with young babies. They can be secured along the side of the pram or changing table when the baby is being massaged after the bath or when he is having his nappy changed.

- Other books that show colourful single objects or faces will be popular. Even very young babies will show an interest in simple lift-the-flap books like *Spot the Dog*.

- Rattles made of fabric that are soft and light to handle are very popular with babies over four months. Choose brightly coloured ones with smiling faces.

- A baby mirror is another toy that babies seem to love. There are double sided ones available with a mirror on one side and black, white and red designs on the reverse.

- There are a variety of colourful soft toys designed to squeak, rattle or rustle. They are usually made from different types of fabric, encouraging awareness of texture. The most popular ones are an octopus, a snake and a clown that wobbles.

Babies of all ages will benefit from hearing different types of music and they enjoy being danced with. There are also many organised classes – massage, swimming and baby gym are just a few that most young babies seem to enjoy. Check with your local library for details of classes in your area. Toys and classes are not the only way to relieve your baby's boredom. Even the youngest babies will enjoy the atmosphere, noise and activity of a trip to the local museum, art gallery and even supermarket.

Babies over six months can get particularly frustrated and bored. Unlike the younger baby they will not be content to lie for 20 minutes or so under the cot mobile or on the activity mat.

Listed below are some of the toys that are popular with babies over six months. Always check that the toys conform to British Standard BS5665.

- Colourful balls are a great hit with older babies. Some have several buttons that, when pressed, make different sounds. Others are clear with an object inside that wobbles when the ball is rolled.
- Activity centres that fix to the side of the cot or playpen are designed to help develop a baby's manual skills. They have a selection of dials, buttons and bells that make different sounds and some incorporate a musical device. The one that is designed to look like a teddy bear is very popular.
- Baby bouncers that are suspended from a door or special frame are excellent for older babies who have enough neck control to support their heads.
- Soft activity toys such as snakes, crocodiles and birds designed to squeak, crinkle, rattle and make different noises are great for a multi-sensory experience.
- Stacker toys with different stackable shapes will help develop your baby's hand and wrist control. Choose one that is brightly coloured and where each shape has a different texture and makes a different sound.

Overstimulation

Rarely a day goes by without an article being published on the importance and benefits to babies and children of being properly stimulated. Parents are told they should talk to their baby all the time and read books from an early age. They are also advised to enrol their baby in different classes and buy a variety of toys. All of these things are supposed to make a happier and brighter baby.

I totally agree with this advice and believe that babies can benefit enormously from all of the things mentioned above. However, I also believe care should be taken that the baby's waking time does not become overloaded. Stimulation and activities must be fitted around feeding and sleeping times. Failure to get the right balance will result in the baby becoming overstimulated. An overstimulated baby will quickly become an overtired baby who will then cry endlessly as he fights sleep. To ensure that your baby does not become overstimulated and overtired take a cue from how long he can stay awake. Allow a minimum 15 minutes wind-down time before his day-time sleep and 30 minutes before bed-time. I find it helps to have wake-up toys and wind-down toys. For example, I would use the cot mobile, baby gym and other musical toys for wakeful periods. During the wind-down times I would use the cot mirror and certain books or a soft toy.

Anxiety

By the age of six months babies begin to realise they are separate from their mothers and a baby may show signs of separation anxiety or stranger anxiety. The happy contented baby who was so easy-going and relaxed and who would go to anyone suddenly becomes clingy, anxious and demanding. He screams if his mother leaves the room for even a few minutes and often gets hysterical if approached by a stranger. This behaviour is a totally normal part of a baby's development. All babies will go through this stage to some degree, usually somewhere between six and 12 months. In my experience babies who are used to being with someone else on a regular basis usually suffer less from separation anxiety.

If your baby suddenly becomes more clingy around this age it is important to understand that he is not being naughty or demanding. Forcing him to go to strangers or leaving him alone in a room to play by himself will not solve the problem and may lead him to become more fretful and insecure. Responding quickly and positively to his anxiety rather than ignoring it will, in the long run, help him become more confident and independent.

Although this stage can be very exhausting for a mother, it rarely lasts long. The following guidelines can help make this dif-ficult period less stressful.

- Many babies develop a need for a comforter at this age, usu-ally a special blanket, cloth or toy. Refer to page 137 for advice on comforters.
- If you are planning to return to work when your baby is between six and nine months, it is important to make sure that he gets accustomed to being left with someone else before he reaches six months.
- Get him used to the nursery or childminder at least two weeks before returning to work. Gradually lengthen the period of time you leave him.

- Provided you are confident that your baby is happy with his carer, do not prolong the goodbye. A hug and kiss and reminder that you will be back soon is enough. Using the same approach and words each time you say goodbye will, in the long term, be more reassuring than going back to try and calm him.
- During this period instruct your baby's carer that he must not be subjected to too many different new things at once or to handling by strangers. The calmer and more predictable his routine, the quicker he will get over his feelings of anxiety.
- Try to arrange regular play dates with only a small group of the same mothers and babies. Once he appears to be happier and begins responding to the regular faces, gradually introduce him into larger groups and other new experiences.

Bowel movements

For many babies a bowel movement is accompanied by much grunting, groaning and straining, and often some crying. Concerned parents worry that this is a sign of pain and constipation. In my experience, this behaviour is fairly common in young babies and constipation is rarely the cause, especially with babies under four months. Dr Spock believed the reason for fussing and fretting is that the stools of very young babies are so soft they do not put enough pressure on the anus, making elimination more difficult. There is possibly some truth in this theory, as I usually find when solids are introduced and bowel movements become firmer, crying disappears. A baby suffering from genuine constipation will have irregular bowel movements in the form of small hard pellets. If your baby is crying for excessive lengths of time before and after a bowel movement, seek advice from your doctor or health visitor.

Discomfort

In addition to ensuring a baby's feeding and sleeping needs are met, parents can do much to reduce crying by ensuring that their baby is comfortable. There are many reasons that would cause a baby to cry from discomfort. Particular attention should be given to room temperature, the baby's cot, bedding and sleepwear. Careful thought should also be given to the choice of day-time wear. While a baby may look cute dressed in trendy jogging pants and miniature trainers, they do little for his comfort.

The following are the main causes of discomfort in young babies:

Room temperature

- The ideal room temperature during the day for a young baby is between 20° and 22°C (68° and 72°F) and between 15° and 18°C (60° and 65°F) at night. Allowing a baby to sleep in an overheated room not only contributes to the risk of cot death but also dries the mucus membranes of the nose. This can cause great discomfort to the baby and some medical experts claim it makes them more vulnerable to colds and infection.

- A battery-operated room thermometer is the best way to ensure your baby's room is kept at the correct temperature. Some models are designed with an alarm that will sound if the temperature goes below or above the ideal level.

- The cot should not be positioned near a radiator, window or outside wall. The bedding for the cot should be 100 per cent cotton, and quilts, bumpers and pillows should be avoided as they can cause overheating, which plays a big factor in cot death. If a very young baby is still being swaddled, remember to reduce the layers of bedding on the cot. Gradually get your baby used to not being swaddled by the time he reaches six to eight weeks of age.

- In very hot weather it is advisable during the day to pull down the blind halfway to avoid the room becoming overheated. Babies can get very irritable in hot weather and may benefit from a fan in the room but ensure that it does not blow directly on the baby. Care should be taken to reduce the layers of bedding in hot weather. If a sleeping bag is being used, make sure it is a summer weight bag made of 100 per cent cotton and lined with cotton. On very hot nights a nappy and the very thin bag is usually all the baby needs to wear. If the temperature drops, a thin blanket or sheet can be added.

- The best way to check whether your baby is too hot or cold is to feel the back of his neck. The layers of bedding should then be adjusted accordingly.

- When making up the cot, care should be taken to ensure the sheets and blankets are smooth and not crumpled. They also need to be tucked in securely so they cannot work their way loose or flap against the baby's face.

- Bed linen should be washed at 15°C (60°F) to rid it of house mite droppings, which can cause wheezing in some babies.
- Toys, activity centres and overhead mobiles should all be removed when the baby is asleep in the cot. As the baby comes into light sleep even a very soft toy can cause him to wake if he rolls onto it. The sudden noise of an activity centre accidentally banged will certainly cause the baby to wake up, crying with fright.
- The baby's comfort should be considered when choosing clothing. Babygrows and sleep suits with large buttons at the back or big collars that flap against the baby's face could cause discomfort. Equally, jogging pants with an elasticated waist worn with a bulky nappy will also be uncomfortable.
- Particular attention should be paid to the inside of clothes as loose threads or curled up labels could cause irritation.
- During the winter months, it is important to ensure that a baby does not get overheated in the buggy. When entering warm shops remember to remove his hat and pull back the 'cozy toze'.

Nappy rash

Nappy rash can be extremely painful for a baby and while some babies are more prone to it than others, with vigilance I believe it can be avoided. Frequent nappy changing, especially in hot weather, and proper cleansing of the nappy areas are the keys to avoiding nappy rash.

- Change your baby's nappy every couple of hours regardless of whether he has had a bowel movement.
- Cleanse your baby's bottom using plain, cool, boiled water or a little baby oil and cotton wool. Avoid using baby wipes on very young babies, especially if the bottom area looks red.
- If you use a barrier cream apply only a thin layer. Too much will reduce the absorbency of disposable nappies.
- Never use baby powder. Not only does it clog the skin but even the tiniest amount can prove fatal if it reaches a baby's lungs.
- Remove your baby's nappy and expose his bottom to fresh air at least twice a day.
- If your baby's bottom does become affected, cleaning it will be less painful if unperfumed baby oil and cotton wool are used instead of water or baby wipes.

4

Toddlerhood

I am always curious as to how my clients envisage themselves as parents in the years ahead. One thing that all parents want for their baby is that he grows up to be a healthy, happy and confident adult. During those growing years some of the things they hope he will learn include playing happily with other children, sharing, being polite, well-mannered and generous of spirit. It is quite a long list of expectations for such a small human being, but it is what all parents dream of and come to expect of their baby.

I have never yet heard a parent say 'I don't mind if he turns out to be a spoilt, whingeing toddler, and a jealous, greedy, bad-mannered child'. Yet we have all seen such children. We meet them in the playground, at kiddies' birthday parties, and we all have a good friend with the nightmare toddler.

These children were not born like that – so what went wrong? The blame is often laid on the parents. The older generation say that today's babies and children are far too spoilt, and that a tougher line should be taken from day one. Children should do as they are told – no discussion and no arguments. If we listen to the view of the psychoanalysts, especially those of the Freud school of thought, this approach is the cause of insecurity in children, which results in them becoming unhappy adults.

I do not profess to have all the answers on how to help your 'contented baby' become a 'confident child'. However, over the years my hands-on experience of working and living 24 hours a day with families all over the world has taught me a great deal of what works and what doesn't. I have observed the behaviour, both good and bad, of hundreds of toddlers and young children and also the different ways in which parents deal with their children's difficult behaviour. Some will follow their own parents' strict autocratic approach to discipline; others have a much more liberal approach, taking time to talk, explain and reason with their children. There are also parents who get very distraught about their children's difficult behaviour. Feelings of guilt that their children are displaying emotions other than those of happiness, often lead them to resort to bribery and persuasion, in trying to avoid such confrontations.

Baby to toddler

The majority of babies begin to take their first steps just before their first birthday. These important first steps signify the beginning of a baby's journey into toddlerhood. Once he is walking, his perception of the world around him suddenly changes and his curiosity increases, as he views more things from an upright level. This new-found mobility is a vital stage in the toddler's development as it gives him the independence to explore his surroundings, and the ability to learn other skills. He learns more between the ages of one and three years than at any other time in his life. The learning process often ends up in tears of frustration through not being understood, and sheer exhaustion from having to learn so many different things at the same time. This time often sees the arrival of a new baby, which adds the fear of abandonment and feelings of jealousy to the very long list of emotions with which the toddler is having to cope.

Listed below are just a few of the main skills and challenges a toddler has to deal with.

- Learning to make his needs understood – by talking.
- Learning to become more physically independent – walking, undressing and dressing himself.
- Learning how to make choices on what to eat and how to feed himself.
- Learning bladder and bowel control – by potty training.
- Learning how to integrate with other toddlers – by playing and sharing.
- Learning how to become less dependent on his parents – attending playgroup or nursery.

During this stage of development it is essential that a toddler has a safe, happy and relaxed environment to master these skills confidently. Toddlers soon become very frustrated if they keep hearing the word 'no', or are constantly reminded to be careful, or 'not to touch'.

In my experience, much conflict, many tears and tantrums could be avoided if parents created a home that would allow their toddler to grow up freely and safely, instead of a showcase to display possessions and reflect their success and 'good taste'.

Usually, I can tell very quickly which of my babies will experience more difficulties during their toddler years. I must confess that my prediction, which nearly always turns out to be accurate, has rarely been based on the character of the baby. My analysis is usually based on the character of the parents, and drawn from my experience of living in the home that they have created.

I am not suggesting that the home should be turned into a mini version of Disneyland, but it is essential to 'toddler-proof' it, and move anything hazardous out of reach. There should also be at least one room in the house where the toddler is able to play and explore happily and freely without the risk of hurting himself. It is important that his natural curiosity is not hampered by being constantly nagged to be careful with Mummy's precious china plant-pot holder or not to get dirty finger marks on the lovely, old English white paintwork.

Managing the toddler

Creating a safe, happy and relaxed environment will help increase the toddler's confidence during this critical stage of mental, physical and emotional development. However, there will be times when he becomes so challenged that he finds it difficult to cope. Therefore, it is essential that parents set very clear limits and boundaries for dealing with any difficult behaviour caused by their toddler's frustration.

For example, as adults if we choose to learn how to drive, we place ourselves in the hands of a driving instructor. A good teacher makes the rules and sets the limits, and provides us with a sound framework so that we can learn to drive successfully. He will also show great patience and tolerance as we learn to master both the mental and physical skills needed to drive properly and safely. He will not ridicule or punish us when we make a mistake. However, he would take over the control of the car if we were about to make a mistake that could have serious consequences.

Likewise, it is important that parents show the same patience and tolerance when their toddler is learning the numerous new skills with which he is faced, and when necessary, be prepared to take charge if things appear to be getting out of control. There is very little room for punishment at this stage of child development.

Toddlers, if they are to grow into confident and happy children, need to learn with the minimum of frustration. As adults and teachers it is our responsibility to ensure that we provide our children with a sound framework, and a clear set of rules and limits that help the toddler face the challenge, not that challenge the toddler. The right environment, along with your help and encouragement will make it easier for your toddler to master the following skills.

Walking

While the majority of toddlers are walking soon after their first birthday, it can take several more months of practice to achieve the balance and coordination needed for steady walking. Until this is achieved they do not have the ability to steer themselves properly. During this stage there will be much falling over, and bumping into things, which can lead to frustration and tantrums.

Listed below are suggestions and guidelines that will help to make things easier for your toddler during the early stages of walking.

- Toddlers will find it easier to learn to walk if they go barefoot, as splaying their toes fully enables them to get a better grip. It is also better for muscle tone and the development of the feet. In very cold weather it is better for him to wear socks with non-slip soles when he is walking indoors; even the softest shoes can restrict his growth.

- The first toddling steps are often referred to as 'cruising'. A toddler will begin by walking sideways first. He uses both hands to pull himself up and hold onto the furniture and support himself as he moves around. Arrange sturdy furniture closer together to encourage cruising.

- As his balance improves, he will begin to use only one hand on the furniture for support. Eventually he becomes confident enough to take a couple of unsupported steps between any small gaps in the furniture.

- As his confidence grows he relies less and less on the furniture for support, moving further and further away from it. Eventually he takes three or four unsupported steps forward at a time.

- Once he is capable of taking a few steps forward, a push-along toy can help him learn to balance. At first he will be unable to control the speed, so it is important always to supervise him otherwise he will tend to fall flat as it gets away from him.

- Avoid using the round type of babywalker on wheels. They are responsible for 5,000 accidents a year, and the Chartered Society of Physiotherapists claim they may also hinder physical and mental development. They also advise parents to avoid leaving their toddlers and children in car seats for too long, as it can delay muscle development.

- Once your toddler has been walking properly for about six weeks, he should be measured for his first pair of shoes by a qualified fitter. It is important to invest in a pair of shoes that are both the right length and the right width. Shoes that do not support his feet properly could cause permanent damage.

Talking

The sooner a toddler is able to communicate his needs by talking, the easier it becomes for parents to control frustration and tantrums. Children learn to talk by listening and while it makes sense to spend lots of time talking to your toddler, it is very important that you also give him the opportunity to respond to what you are saying. Communication is a two way thing and should be fun for your toddler. Although you may not understand much of what he is saying, by showing him you are really interested in his attempts at talking will encourage him to talk even more. By 15 months most toddlers are able to say between six and eight words and by 18 months this will have increased to between 20 and 40 words. At two years of age most toddlers are able to string two words together – for example, 'more juice' or 'mummy gone' – and by the time they reach two and a half years most will have a vocabulary of about 200 words. Speech varies greatly from toddler to toddler but if you have any worries or concerns about your child's speech development it is advisable to seek advice from your health visitor or doctor.

The following guidelines will help encourage your toddler to become a confident talker.

- Reading to your child is an excellent way of increasing his vocabulary, pointing things out as you read the story. Try to spend at least two short quiet spells a day reading to your child, avoiding other distractions such as having the television or radio on or answering the telephone.

- When talking to your toddler make sure that you speak slowly and clearly and that he is able to see your mouth movements as you pronounce the words. During the second year it is also better to try and keep sentences shorter and simple. Once your toddler is stringing three and four words together you can lengthen your sentences.

- Do not correct your toddler when he pronounces a word incorrectly as this will only discourage his attempts, instead it is better to repeat the word back to him correctly. For example, if he says 'big tat' instead of 'big cat', it is better to reply by saying 'yes, it's a big black cat' than forcing him to repeat the word cat correctly several times.

- All toddlers love to mimic adults so singing nursery rhymes which involve lots of action and exaggerated facial expression, along with the constant repetition of the same words is a great way to help your toddler's verbal skills.

- Discuss things as you are doing them with your toddler and emphasise the key words in the sentence. Avoid using pronouns like your or it; for example, 'Let's put on James' red shoes' or 'Where's James' blue ball?' is better than 'Let's put on your shoes' or 'Where is it?'.

- It is worthwhile making a list of any new words you notice your toddler using and making sure that they are introduced as much as possible into the conversations you and the rest of the family have with him.

- Finally, as your toddler's vocabulary increases, be prepared to repeat yourself over and over again as he constantly asks the same questions over and over again. This is all part of your child learning how to talk and the more patient you are when answering his questions the more eager he will be to communicate.

Dressing

By the age of 14 months most toddlers have learned how to pull off their hat and their socks. This is an excellent time to introduce activity toys that will help your toddler develop his manipulation skills. Shape sorter toys, and dolls that come with zips, toggles, buttons etc, will all help him to do this.

It is important to allow extra time once your toddler is learning this skill. He will need lots of encouragement, and will quickly sense if you are in a hurry and become impatient.

- Between 18 and 24 months, the majority of toddlers will be able to remove most of their clothes, and by 30 months most are capable of getting totally undressed and dressed, but will need help with buttons, poppers and braces.
- Your toddler will be less likely to get frustrated or bored if you teach learn him to undress and dress in stages. Once he is capable of taking off his socks and trousers, move on to him taking off his socks, trousers and pants etc. Use the same approach when teaching him how to dress himself.
- Encourage his independence by allowing him to choose which clothes he wears, but do limit the choice so that you remain in control.

Feeding

A toddler who is still drinking from a bottle and continues to be given lots of puréed and mashed foods during the second year, will be much slower at learning to self-feed. To help develop the pincer grip (forefinger and thumb grasp) necessary for confident self-feeding it is essential to introduce lots of finger foods and chopped fruit and vegetables. Feeding bottles should be abandoned by the age of one year, and apart from breast feeds, all other drinks should be given from a non-spill type beaker or cup.

- Between 12 and 15 months most toddlers will attempt to use a spoon, although they will need help with loading it and directing it into their mouth.
- By 18 months a toddler who has had enough practice will manage to eat most of his food by himself using a spoon. Self-feeding with a spoon will be made easier for a toddler if the food is in a bowl.
- At two years of age a toddler should have developed enough hand-eye coordination to eat his food with a small fork and should manage to eat all of his meal without assistance. Toddlers will learn to use their cutlery sooner if they are allowed to join in some family meals and encouraged to copy the adults.

Tantrums

The above skills are just the main ones that a toddler has to learn during his second year, and it will be inevitable that there are times when he gets so frustrated that he feels unable to cope. Just as an electrical circuit will blow a fuse when the system is overloaded, the toddler whose emotions become overloaded with frustration and anger will also blow a fuse; this is referred to as a tantrum. Tantrums are a normal part of a child's development; they are his way of communicating to his parents that he can't manage.

They usually start around the first birthday, which coincides with the time most children begin to walk, they reach a peak around the second birthday (hence the phrase the 'terrible twos'), and by the third birthday they are on the decline. A child having a full-blown tantrum will shout and scream hysterically, throw himself around the room or on the floor, kicking out at anything he can. Severe tantrums like this are very stressful for both the child and the parents, and action should be taken to prevent this sorts of tantrum becoming a regular occurrence.

During this critical stage of your toddler's development, with so many new skills to master, he is likely to get very frustrated. Therefore, it is essential that social activities and sleep are carefully structured so that he doesn't become overtired. In my experience, toddlers and children who are allowed to become overtired are much more prone to having full-blown temper tantrums, than those whose activities and sleep are carefully structured. Prevention is better than cure, and understanding the causes of tantrums will go a long way in helping your toddler to avoid them.

Listed below are the main causes of frustration that can lead to temper tantrums.

- The toddler has the mental capacity to understand virtually everything that is said to him, but does not yet have the verbal skills necessary to communicate how he feels or what he really wants.
- His desire to become more independent will lead him to attempt physical tasks beyond his capabilities.
- A toddler will eat exactly the amount he needs to satisfy his hunger, but being forced to eat just one more spoonful to satisfy the parent's perception of what he needs is sure to lead to a tantrum.
- A child who has too many toys, watches too many videos or attends too many activity classes, will cease to use his imagination and quickly becomes bored if he is not entertained the whole time. Boredom quickly turns into frustration if his demands to be entertained are not met immediately.
- Lengthy shopping trips with toddlers nearly always end in tears. If possible arrange for a friend with a toddler to watch

both of them for a couple of hours, while you do your big shop. This can be reciprocated later.

- Think twice before using the word 'no'. Overuse of the word can result in it not having the desired effect when you really do mean it.
- Both parents should work by the same set of rules, otherwise the toddler will become confused as to what is acceptable behaviour and what is not.

Dealing with tantrums

The above measures can help reduce the number of tantrums a toddler has, and prevent them from becoming a serious habit. However, when feelings of anger, jealousy, fear and frustration get too much, there is bound to be a tantrum, as it is the way in which your toddler will express the inner turmoil that he is feeling. He is not trying to annoy you, nor being deliberately naughty and should not be punished. How to deal with the situation depends very much on his age and the reason for the tantrum, but it is important that he is neither punished nor rewarded.

Listed below are guidelines that will help you deal with your toddler's tantrums.

Diversion

The majority of parents I know believe that diversion is one of the best methods of dealing with a tantrum. In order for distraction to be effective you must get his attention at the beginning of the tantrum, before he has worked himself up into a frenzy. The following three distractions are the ones that I have found to be the most effective.

a) The majority of toddlers love playing with water, so get your toddler to wash the baby's bottles or some plastic containers. If it is close to a meal time get him to help you wash some of the vegetables and fruit. On a warm day suggest that he helps you water the garden.

b) Keep a small selection of balloons, party hats and poppers at hand, and bring them out when you see he is about to throw a wobbly. Alternatively give him one of the small bubble-blowing kits to play with; they can keep some children happy for ages.

c) Some parents keep a slab of ready-made pastry in the fridge and suggest a spot of baking when they notice their toddler is about to lose it. All the pounding and squeezing of the dough soon gets rid of excess frustration.

Time out

Time out is the next most popular method used by parents when distraction fails and a child is having a full-blown temper tantrum. Placing him in his cot with the door shut for a short period of time is a particularly effective way of dealing with a toddler who decides to throw a tantrum in front of grandparents, relatives or friends, whose well-meaning interventions usually make matters worse.

Holding time

A small number of parents say that holding their toddler closely and firmly and talking to him in a soothing tone of voice until he calms down can sometimes work. In my experience this can work only if he has not already worked himself up into a rage, if he is small and easy to grab hold of, or a sensitive toddler and not very strong willed.

Withdraw attention

Some parents believe that the best way to deal with their toddler's tantrum is to let it run its course and totally ignore it. If necessary, go to another room so that the child realises he is no longer the centre of attention. I have occasionally seen this approach work but it has always been in families who are fortunate enough to have child-safe play-rooms in full veiw of the kitchen. It may be worthwhile trying to ignore your child but it is important that he is not left in a situation where he could harm himself.

Aggressive behaviour

The majority of toddlers will occasionally use some form of aggressive behaviour, such as hitting, kicking, biting or scratching. In my experience, toddlers who resort to this sort of aggressive behaviour usually do so when they are feeling insecure. Some feel resentful and jealous when they suddenly find they have to share their parents' attention with a new baby, or share the toys with other children at playgroup. A toddler who has not yet learned to share may try to retrieve his toy from another by kicking. The mother breast feeding the new baby may be subjected to a sudden bite from a toddler who is feeling neglected. A gentle stroke of the baby's cheek by the toddler may end up as a very severe scratch.

Although all of these spur-of-the-moment attacks are intentional, they are not planned and the toddler does not yet understand what causes him to make them. Unlike tantrums, which are usually only directed at the parents, aggressive behaviour can often be directed at anyone whom the toddler feels is a threat. The toddler who gets into the habit of using aggressive behaviour as a way of asserting himself or of getting undivided attention will quickly become very unpopular with other parents and children.

The following guidelines give suggestions on how to deal with a toddler's aggressive behaviour.

- A toddler must learn that aggressive behaviour in any form is not acceptable. Therefore, it is foolish to deal with this problem by smacking him, or even worse, as some books suggest, 'biting him back'.
- If your toddler lashes out aggressively one way or another, immediately take him to one side and explain simply and firmly that biting, hitting etc is not allowed. But avoid using words like 'bad' or 'naughty', which will only make him feel more insecure.
- Reinforce his good behaviour with lots of encouragement and praise, with much emphasis on the times he plays nicely with the baby or other toddlers.
- Be extra vigilant when he is in group situations, and quickly divert his attention when he shows signs of frustration and irritability.
- A toddler should never be left alone with a baby for even a few minutes, and when they are together, they should be kept in full view.

The following scenario is one that I have witnessed many times over the years, and describes how a temper tantrum can evolve and result in aggressive behaviour. The (perhaps natural) response of the mother, I believe, only added to the problem instead of addressing it.

Mother, Alexander (aged 23 months) and baby William (aged four weeks) are all in the sitting room. Baby William is just finishing off his breast feed which takes about 35 minutes. During this time Alexander behaves perfectly, playing with his toys and chatting happily to his mother. His mother makes a particular point of repeatedly telling

Alexander what a good boy he is, and how much his baby brother loves him. She constantly encourages Alexander to stroke the baby's head, impressing the importance of being very gentle and loving with William.

MOTHER: *Alexander, why don't you tidy away your toys while Mummy changes William?*

She lays William on his changing mat on the floor while she gets the changing things.

ALEXANDER: *No, don't want.*

MOTHER: *If you put your toys away quickly Mummy will give you a nice biscuit.*

Alexander then starts to whinge and stamp his feet as he proceeds to throw his toys across the room, aiming for the toy box. The commotion sets the baby off crying and the mother begins to get fraught.

MOTHER: *Alexander, be careful putting your toys away, one may accidently hit your brother and hurt him.*

Alexander promptly throws a small ball at his baby brother, hitting him on the head. The baby screams with fright, and the mother screams at William.

MOTHER: *You bad boy, you're very naughty, you've made poor baby William cry. If you ever do that again I will take all your toys away, and there will be no more biscuits.*

Alexander starts screaming and throwing his toys everywhere.

ALEXANDER: *Don't want toys, don't want biscuit, no baby, no Mummy.*

Within minutes a happy family scene has turned into an uncontrollable situation of anger, jealousy, whingeing, bribery, threats, fear and frustration.

The mother then attempts to calm the situation down. She cuddles the sobbing Alexander and gives him the biscuit which he was promised if he had put his toys away nicely. She explains how much she loves him and that she knows he really is a good little boy and that good little boys must not throw their toys around and be nasty to people. Alexander at this stage doesn't really care whether he is called good, bad or naughty because he was now getting what he wanted all along; love, cuddles and attention from Mummy.

Many things could have been done to help avoid the situation in the first place. If we go through the whole scenario again step by step we can look at what prompted Alexander's behaviour and the way in which one can avoid or at least minimise potential problems in this type of situation.

The mother, aware that the baby's feed would take at least 30–40 minutes, was anxious that Alexander should remain calm and happy throughout the feed. She settled him with his toys and from the start gave Alexander lots of praise. Modern-day psychology places great emphasis on praising good behaviour and ignoring bad, and getting the older baby involved with a new baby from the outset. In theory this seems sound advice, but unfortunately all too often, as in Alexander's case, it backfires. While Alexander appeared to be happy and content playing with his toys while his mother fed the baby, I am sure that after 15–20 minutes his boredom threshold was reducing. He was more than likely not feeling like the good boy his mother kept insisting he was, and fed up with having constantly to admire the baby.

By the time the feed was coming to an end he was feeling very bored and frustrated and he wanted some individual attention from his mother. The thought of having to clear away his toys and wait until his mother changed the baby's nappy to get a cuddle and a biscuit probably seemed too far away.

He wanted things to be like they were before the baby came along – for Mummy to be there when he needed her, not having to share her with this very demanding other person. In his eyes, if the baby could scream and get his mother's immediate attention, then that is the way he would get it as well. At 23 months of age, and with a new baby brother he was experiencing many new emotions. When placed in a situation where several of these emotions surfaced at the same time, he dealt with this in the only way he knew. The feeding of a young baby can take anything up to one hour, which is a long time for a child of Alexander's age.

By planning and thinking ahead, the outburst could well have been avoided.

The following guidelines and suggestions explain how to cope with a toddler and feeding a new baby at the same time, and hopefully avoid a temper tantrum.

- At the beginning of the feed Alexander was perfectly happy. At that stage the mother would have been better advised to get on with feeding the baby, and not draw attention to him.

- Alexander should have been allowed to decide for himself if he wanted to admire and talk to the baby, not constantly be forced to do so.
- The mother would have done better to change the baby's nappy midway through the feed. By saying 'let's go and get some water for William's nappy change and a biscuit and some juice for you', she could have distracted Alexander enough to prevent him from getting bored near the end of the feed.
- Once the baby had finished feeding and with the nappy already changed, the mother could have put the baby straight into his chair, knowing that all his needs had been met; the physical contact of holding and cuddling him during the feed, his hunger satisfied and a clean nappy. She would then have been able to give some much needed and undivided attention to Alexander, while making a game of the two of them clearing the toys away.
- Finally, it is worth remembering that it is pointless trying to reason with a distraught toddler about why he shouldn't hate his baby brother. At this point he is too emotional. The only rule that should have been made clear is that no matter how he feels towards his brother, he is without question never allowed to hurt him.
- Toy chests and baskets are always a potential danger. Different toys should have been stored in different boxes, preferably with securely fitting lids, and kept in a cupboard with a door that shuts. This way the mother can ensure that only the safe toys are brought out when the baby is around. (See page 139 for advice on toy storage.)
- Balls should never be allowed in the house; children should learn from the very earliest age that certain toys and games are for outside play only. It avoids situations like the one that I have just described, when a second baby arrives.
- The word 'if' is best avoided with small children as it usually results in parents trying to bribe the child into good behaviour. The child soon begins to believe that the only reason for good behaviour is the reward at the end of it.

When a new baby comes along I think that parents should accept that some degree of jealousy is normal and to be expected. How parents deal with the jealousy is another matter, and as I have mentioned, today's childcare experts put great emphasis on the importance of constantly praising the toddler and involving him in the care of the baby. While the majority of children respond well to the praise, the overuse of praise to improve difficult behaviour can backfire.

Problems with praise

Parents use praise to show their children they approve of things they consider to be well done. The problem with this is that the praise is based solely on the parents' judgement and evaluation of the child's behaviour. It leaves no room for the child's point of view. Jane Nelson, psychologist and mother of seven children, believes that the overuse of praise to improve behaviour can result in children becoming pleasers and approval 'junkies'. In her book *Positive Discipline* she explains how these children (and later these adults) develop self-concepts that are totally dependent on the opinions of others. Other children, she claims, can resent and rebel against praise, either because they don't want to live up to the expectations of others or because they fear they can't compete with those who seem to get praise so easily. The long-term effect of praise is often that a child becomes too dependent on others.

Nelson believes that encouragement is preferable to praise, as it takes into consideration the child's point of view, inspiring self-evaluation that will lead to a child becoming more self-confident and independent. While I still think praise is an important tool of parenthood, it should be used with caution. Since reading this excellent book I have come to agree with the author that encouragement, along with praising the actual deed rather than the child himself, is the most effective way to improve behaviour.

To try and understand how a child may perceive praise, think of how we as adults feel when we receive praise. For example, we can all remember a time when we spent hours preparing for a special dinner party for a partner or close friend, and the amount of hard work it takes to shop, prepare and cook the perfect meal and then present the meal and yourself to the best of your ability. As the guests bid their farewells and thank you for the splendid evening, which of the comments from a partner would mean more to you?

Example one: 'You're such a star. I am so lucky to have such a great wife/husband, I don't know what I would do without you. You looked beautiful and, as always, got everything right, I am so proud of you.'

Example two: 'Thank you for making the evening such a success, I really appreciate all the time and effort you put into cooking such a fantastic meal. I think everyone enjoyed the evening. How about you, did you enjoy yourself?'

Example one is all based on the husband's perception of what he expects from his wife and how she should look, act and behave. On receiving the compliment, it is hardly likely that the wife thought: Yes, I am a star and very beautiful, and you're very lucky to have me as I am always capable of getting everything right. She probably felt very patronised and like a trophy wife under a great deal of pressure to live up to her husband's expectations.

Example two takes into consideration not only the hard work that the wife has put into the dinner party, but also the husband's concern about whether she also enjoyed herself. Example two is based on appreciation, respect and empathy, unlike example one which is based on direct praise of personality.

Sibling rivalry: jealousy

Sibling rivalry is not something that is new to today's parents – it has existed since the beginning of time. Prime examples are in The Bible: Cain slaying his brother Abel; Joseph suffering at the hands of his brothers, first thrown into the snake pit, then being sold to a life of slavery in the desert. The reason then was probably not very different from today: that of jealousy. A new baby represents a threat to the elder children, especially first children who have enjoyed the undivided love and attention of their parents. The child or children have to come to terms with loss of the parents' time which can often lead to the toddler or child feeling very insecure, resulting in all sorts of what the parents consider to be unreasonable behaviour.

Many books and baby magazines give advice on how to prepare a toddler or child for the arrival of a new baby. A lot of emphasis is placed on reading one of the many books specially written for children about the arrival of a new baby. Mothers are also told to encourage their toddlers to speak to the baby in the womb, and to allow them to help prepare the nursery. This is all good advice, but personally I feel that many unfortunate situations could be avoided by establishing the correct rules and guidelines for the toddler or child well in advance of the arrival of the new baby.

The following scenario explains how the importance of clear and firm limits for young toddlers can help avoid some of the very many difficult situations that so many parents experience when a new baby arrives.

Thomas, aged 15 months, is playing in his parents' bedroom – a ritual that takes place every Sunday morning. Thomas, crawling but not yet walking, has a great fascination with Daddy's tennis and squash balls which are stored behind a large armchair. He plays happily for 20 minutes or so rolling the balls back and forth to his parents (his mother is three months pregnant) who take this opportunity to lie and relax on the bed while reading the Sunday papers. Occasionally, Thomas manages to aim a ball so it lands on his parents bed. They gently throw the ball back, stressing the importance of throwing it gently. Both Thomas and his parents get much pleasure out of this little ritual.

However, try to imagine the scene six months down the line when the new baby has joined the parents on the bed. Thomas, now 21 months, is walking and much stronger. He is unlikely to be satisfied with just rolling the balls and much more likely to attempt to throw and toss them in the air. The parents' attempt suddenly to try and stop the ritual that had gone on for many months only leads to Thomas getting very upset. Their repeated warning to Thomas to be careful when he is rolling the balls have no effect, and the inevitable happens – the baby gets hit by a flying ball, resulting in screams all round. The shocked and worried parents, while trying to console the crying baby, lose their tempers with Thomas (who is now also screaming) calling him 'naughty' and 'careless'.

Whether Thomas threw the ball at the baby on purpose we will never know, and it is not the issue of the story. The issue is whether he should ever have been allowed to play with the balls in the bedroom in the first place. To me this is a typical example of unclear limits being set for a child. It was ridiculous ever to expect the child to be satisfied with throwing the ball gently – balls are not designed for gentle play. Therefore the parents' expectation of Thomas playing gently with the ball in the bedroom was unrealistic. Yet again, this is a case of limits between outside play and inside play not being set properly.

When deciding on rules and limits for toddlers, parents would do well to think in advance of the time when a new baby will arrive and whether the rules and limits they are setting now will be realistic then.

Routine and rituals

Before the new baby arrives you should look closely at your toddler's routine, especially any rituals that take place in the morning and at bedtime Try to make changes that you think will need to be made well in advance, so that your toddler does not see the arrival of the baby as the cause of the changes in his life. For example, if he is used to sitting on your knee for his bedtime story, try to get him used to sitting next to you instead. This will make it possible for you to feed the baby at the same time as you are reading him his story. Meal times may need to be altered slightly to fit in with breast feeding, as will the time of the bath.

Listed below are further suggestions on how to prepare your toddler for the arrival of a new baby, and an example of how a contented little baby routine can fit in with a toddler's routine.

- The more skills your toddler has learned before the baby arrives the easier it will be for you to cope with the demands of two children. The majority of toddlers are capable of self-feeding by 18 months and undressing themselves by 30 months. A toddler who is still dependent on you to help him with these things will get very resentful if you expect him suddenly to start to do them for himself after the baby is born.
- Try to get your toddler used to entertaining himself for short spells while you do necessary chores. Introduce play activities such as jigsaws, drawing, finger painting and play dough. Both boys and girls will benefit from having their own special baby

doll, complete with feeding bottle, nappies, bath and Moses basket.

- Avoid major changes in your toddler's life prior to the birth or after the baby is born. It can take several weeks for a toddler to settle into nursery, so try to organise his starting date either several weeks before the birth or several weeks after the baby has arrived. If you need his cot for the new baby, try to put him in his new bed at least two months before the baby arrives. (Refer to page 107 for advice on the big bed).

- Try to arrange that your husband and toddler get used to having short spells alone together at the weekend. This way your toddler will not feel you are suddenly abandoning him, when you have much needed rest during the early weeks of breast feeding.

- Get your toddler used to babies by inviting friends with babies to visit. Discuss how small and fragile they are, also how noisy they can be when they cry. Read books that explain about babies being born and having a new baby in the family.

Food fights

During the first year, a baby will grow rapidly and most babies will have increased their height by 50 per cent and tripled their birth weight by the time they reach their first birthday. In the second year, growth slows down and there is often a very noticeable decrease in the toddler's appetite. Elizabeth Morse says in her book *My Child Won't Eat*, 'If a child grew at the same rate as in the first year, he would be 29 metres long and weigh 200 tonnes by the age of ten'. Unfortunately, many parents are not aware that the decrease in their toddler's appetite is normal. They become anxious that he is not eating enough and often resort to spoonfeeding him in the vain hope that it will get his old appetite back. Unfortunately, the pressure to get the toddler to eat more usually has the opposite effect and results in what many childcare experts term 'food fights'. Meal times soon become a battleground, with the toddler screaming as his parents insist on him having just one more spoonful. If you wish to avoid these feeding problems with your toddler, or if he is already experiencing them, it is essential that you have a clear understanding of what he needs to eat for a healthy and well-balanced diet. This will help avoid food fights and fussy eating and will also encourage long-term healthy eating habits.

Encouraging good eating habits

Meal times should be happy and relaxed occasions, but with children under two years old it is unfair to expect them to eat without some degree of mess. At this stage, as long as a toddler is eating well and enjoying his food, no comment should be made about any mess that he may make. However, if he starts playing with his food and throwing it on the floor, it is best to assume that he is not hungry and remove his plate.

Forcing a toddler to eat when he is not really hungry will only create a more serious problem. This can be avoided if you ensure that your toddler's daily intake of food and drink is properly structured. A toddler who becomes overtired, or overhungry, will behave in the same way as the overtired or overhungry baby – he will not eat well. Therefore, it is important to be consistent with the timing of meals. In my experience, breakfast should be finished by 8am, so that the toddler is ready to eat a good lunch at around 12 noon and finally tea at no later than 5pm. Snacks should always be given midway between meals, as even the smallest amount of food or drink can take the edge off the toddler's appetite. A toddler who is having breakfast around 7.30am should be offered a mid-morning snack and drink between 9.30am and 10am, and a mid-afternoon snack and drink no later than 3pm.

A sample menu for an 18-month toddler should look something like this:

Breakfast   7.30-8am
1 cup of full-fat organic milk
50g (2oz) cereal with milk and chopped fruit
small organic yoghurt
small slice of buttered toast

Mid-Morning   9.30-10am
1 cup of well-diluted juice or water
1 small piece of fruit

Lunch   12 noon
50g (2oz) of chicken or white fish
2 small broccoli or cauliflower florets

½ chopped carrot or 1 baby corn
1 tablespoon of peas
1 cup of well-diluted juice or water

Mid-afternoon   3pm
1 cup of well-diluted juice or water
1 small piece of fruit, rice cake or plain cookie

Tea   5pm
Pasta with a tablespoon of mixed vegetables and sauce
1 small chopped apple with yoghurt or cheese
1 small cup of milk, well-diluted juice or water

Bedtime   7-7.30pm
1 cup of full-fat organic milk

Very important: Fruit juice should always be well diluted and ideally given at meal times as this reduces the possibility of damage to your toddler's teeth. Try to restrict juice to no more than two cups per day.

Food refusal

It is vital that meal times do not become a battle of the wills. How you deal with any feeding problems at this stage may affect your toddler's attitude to food for the rest of his life. In my experience, toddlers who are going through a fussy stage and who are constantly coaxed, bribed or force-fed by spoon, nearly always end up with a long-term eating problem.

If you are concerned that your toddler may not be eating enough, it would be a good thing to keep a food diary for one week. Each day list all the food and drink he has taken, as well as the times of consumption. Because his appetite can vary considerably from day to day, it is important that you calculate your toddler's overall food intake over one week. Most parents find that over several days the amount of food their toddler has eaten averages out to meet all his nutritional requirements. However, if your toddler's food diary shows that he is actually eating less than the recommended amounts, it would be advisable to discuss things with your doctor or health visitor.

I have listed below the most common causes of food refusal and faddiness, and some guidelines which encourage good eating habits, and help avoid long-term problems.

- Drinking excessive amounts of milk is a major cause of a toddler refusing to eat. They need a minimum of 350ml (11½oz), and a maximum of 600ml (20oz), per day (inclusive of milk used in food). The bottle should be abandoned at one year, and after that all milk drinks should be given in a beaker or a cup.
- Fruit juice given immediately before food, or within an hour prior to eating can take the edge off a toddler's appetite. Encourage your toddler to eat half of his food before giving him the drink. If possible try to get your toddler used to drinking water in between meals. If juice is given make sure it is very well-diluted, and offer it no later than two hours before his meal time.
- Many leading brands of fromage frais are high in sugar, containing sometimes as much as 14.5g (½oz) in a 100g (4oz) pot. Sugar is often the second largest ingredient in the pot. Toddlers can become addicted to these and if given them often enough, will soon lose their appetite for other foods.
- Try to offer a variety of different foods in small amounts, rather than one or two in large amounts. For example, serving fish with a small amount of carrots, cauliflower, peas and potatoes is more likely to stimulate the toddler's taste buds than serving fish with carrots and potatoes. By offering him a selection of the foods you know he likes, he can be encouraged at least to try some of them.
- It is best to serve your toddler's main protein meal at lunch time, then if he becomes fussy and tired later in the day, you know he has had one good meal and you can be more relaxed about tea. He can then be offered something quick and easy like pasta or baked potato with a filling, or a thick soup and sandwiches.
- Schedule meals and snacks at regular times and stick to these times. If after 30 minutes your toddler is not showing any interest in eating, remove the food without making any comment on his lack of appetite. However, he should not be allowed anything to eat or drink until the next scheduled meal or snack. Ideally there should be a two-hour gap between meals and snacks.

- Giving even the smallest of snacks less than two hours before a meal can be enough to affect some toddlers' appetites, as can the type of snack given. Foods that take longer to digest will be more likely to take the edge off your toddler's appetite.
- Avoid giving your toddler puddings or sweets as an incentive for finishing his meal. This only leads him to think that the food can't be that good, if you are offering him a bribe to eat it. Instead, offer a selection of fresh fruit, cheese and crackers, or plain yoghurt mixed with mashed fresh fruit.
- Try to avoid distractions at meal times such as reading or playing games. Also remember that every time you speak to your toddler, he will need to answer. Therefore be careful about getting into long-winded conversations before he has managed to eat most of his meal.

Sleeping problems

Even the most contented little baby who has always slept well during his first year can suddenly develop sleep problems during the second. There are several reasons why a toddler, who as a baby always settled well at bedtime and slept through the night, suddenly refuses to go to sleep or wakes several times a night. A very common reason is that parents often miss the signs that he is ready to cut back on the amount of sleep he needs during the day, which can result in night-time problems. At one year most babies are still having an average of 14–15 hours of sleep a day, divided between night-time sleep and two day-time naps. However, as he enters toddlerhood the amount of sleep needed is reduced to an average of 13–14 hours a day, which is usually divided between night-time sleep and one day-time nap. Watching for the signs that your toddler is ready to cut back on his sleep can help avoid night-time sleep problems evolving.

The following signs are an indication that your toddler is probably ready to cut down on his hours of daily sleep.

- The majority of toddlers will show signs of cutting back their sleep between the ages of 15 months and 18 months.
- He may take longer and longer to drop off to sleep when put down for his nap at 9.30am, or may still settle well but cut the amount of time he sleeps down to 15–20 minutes.

- He sleeps well at the morning nap, but cuts right back on his lunch-time nap.
- He takes longer to settle and sleep in the evening, or begins to wake up earlier in the morning.

By watching for the above signs you will be able to structure your toddler's day-time sleep, to ensure that his night-time sleep is not affected. During the second year, it becomes easier to adapt the original routine and many parents can get into the habit of being relaxed about timing. Structuring your toddler's sleep is still very important if you wish to avoid him becoming overtired, which in turn can lead to sleep problems.

The following changes to the original 7am–7pm routine will need to be made sometime during the second year, as your toddler shows signs of cutting back on his sleep. I also give suggestions how to adapt things should you wish to change the times of the original routines.

The 7am–7pm routine

A baby who has been following the original 7am–7pm routine to the letter, will normally cut back on the early morning nap first. He will take longer and longer to drop off to sleep when he is put down for his nap at 9–9.30am. If your baby reaches a stage where he is only sleeping for 10–15 minutes at this time, and getting through happily to his lunch-time nap you could cut it out altogether.

The majority of toddlers would then continue to need a full two-hour sleep in the middle of the day, until they are almost two years of age. Occasionally, some toddlers start to cut back on their lunch-time nap at around 18 months. They may sleep for two hours some days and only 1½ hours on other days.

If your toddler does not sleep the full two hours but seems happy in his cot, I would advise you not to rush to him. A toddler who is used to quiet time alone, will eventually learn how to relax and recharge without sleep. This can be a great help when he gets older and drops his nap altogether.

The 8am–7pm routine

Many parents use this routine when their baby reaches one year. Others will use the 7am–7pm during the week and the 8am–7pm routine at the weekend if they want a lie in. Obviously it will only work if your toddler is still having to be woken at 7am, or if he will resettle himself back to sleep fairly quickly if he does wake at 7am. The darker the room, the more likely this is to happen. A toddler under 18 months who sleeps until 8am should not be allowed a morning nap, even if he normally has one on the 7am–7pm routine. His lunch would need to be brought forward slightly, so that he could go down for his two-hour nap not much later than 12.30pm, and be ready for bed at 7pm. A toddler over 18 months who sleeps until 8am would probably manage to get through to 1pm, and then have a nap of no longer than 1½ hours if you wanted him to be ready for bed at 7pm.

7am–7.30/8pm

This routine is often used by working parents who want to spend a little extra time with their toddler on their return from work. It can work for many toddlers, but there is a greater risk of over-tiredness becoming a problem. To avoid this happening, the toddler should still be encouraged to have a nap in the morning, no matter how short. This would help him to get through to 1pm, when hopefully he would sleep for two hours. The short morning nap and the later lunch-time nap should help him manage to get through happily to the later bedtime of 7.30–8pm. If you find that your toddler is getting incredibly tired on this routine, try alternating his bedtime so he is in bed slightly earlier every second night.

Longer morning nap

Often a toddler will show no signs of giving up his morning nap, and will actually cut back on the lunch-time nap. This suits some mothers as it allows them to get many more chores done in the morning if they do not have a toddler in tow. The problem with encouraging a longer nap at this time, is that once the toddler is only having one nap a day, he will be awake right through from 12noon–7pm. Some toddlers eventually get so exhausted by the evening that they fall straight into a very deep sleep the minute they are in bed. This usually has a knock-on effect of the toddler waking earlier in the morning. The earlier waking means that he will become tired earlier, and that the nap time comes even earlier. A vicious circle soon emerges where the toddler is starting his day at 6am or earlier.

Bedtime battles

The toddler who refuses to go to bed is a very common problem. This often coincides with the arrival of a new baby. In my experience, the main reason that this happens is because the mother does not anticipate how much longer everything will take trying to settle two children.

What used to be a calm and happy event often begins to resemble a battleground as an exhausted mother tries to cope with both the toddler and the baby screaming. Obviously the baby's needs and crying has to be attended to first, which means the toddler has even more time to become frustrated and overtired. By the time the baby is settled, the toddler has become so overtired that it can take hours to settle him.

The following guidelines give suggestions on how to plan and prepare a stress-free bedtime for two children, or a toddler who is difficult to settle.

- Try to ensure that your toddler has his main protein meal of the day at lunch-time. This means that tea can be something quick and easy to prepare, like pasta or a thick soup with sandwiches.
- As the children are waking up from their midday nap, lay out everything that is needed for the bath and bedtime. Towels, cotton wool, flannels, nightwear, nappies, bibs, muslins etc, should all be put in the places where they are to be used.
- During the afternoon do not allow your toddler to keep taking different toys out of the cupboard, if he has not tidied away the ones he has finished with. Encourage him to tidy away all or at least some of his toys.
- Tea should be ready and your toddler seated at 5pm sharp, so that you can sit down and feed the baby at the same time as your toddler is eating his tea.
- Both children should be taken upstairs no later than 5.45pm, to allow plenty of time for the bath, and for winding down.
- Try to have both children bathed and dressed by 6.15pm to allow enough time for the baby to take the second half of his feed. Do not allow your toddler to start drinking his milk until you are all settled and ready to watch a video or read a story, while the baby is feeding. Hopefully your toddler will be occu-

pied by drinking his milk and watching the video long enough to allow you to finish feeding the baby.

- Even if the baby does not look tired, settle him in his cot. Dim the lights and prop a small book or mirror down the side of the cot. If this habit is established early enough most babies will learn to settle quickly and easily on their own.
- In the early days most babies will be asleep by 6.30–6.45pm, which should allow you enough time to settle the toddler with his night-time story before he becomes overtired.

The late bedtime

Some toddlers who have been used to a much later bedtime and settled well, may suddenly begin to play up. This usually happens between the ages of 18 months and two years, when his day-time sleep is reduced to one nap, and he is attending more activities during the day. The toddler becomes so overtired, that he ends up fighting sleep for hours. The already late bedtime of 8.30 or 9pm suddenly ends up being 11pm or later. If this is happening with your toddler, it is essential to bring the bedtime forward to avoid him becoming overtired. Provided that overtiredness is the only problem, it should be possible to get your toddler to go to bed earlier, without resorting to controlled crying.

The following guidelines give suggestions on bringing the bedtime forward, and avoiding overtiredness, which results in the toddler being more difficult to settle.

- Try to ensure that your toddler gets plenty of fresh air and exercise during the day. This will help make him more tired and be more likely to need to sleep earlier.
- Avoid noisy games or getting the toddler too excited after tea, and also during and after the bath.
- Do not let your toddler watch a video before the bath. A video after the bath can be used as an incentive to get ready for bed.
- Whatever time your toddler is used to going to bed, bring it forward by 30 minutes to allow enough time to establish the ritual of a drink, a story or video after the bath and teeth cleaning before bed. Remember to dim the lights after the bath.
- Allow three nights to establish the above bedtime ritual, then gradually bring the bedtime forward by ten minutes every three nights.

- Once the bedtime has been brought forward to 7.30pm, con-tinue to be consistent with the ritual after the bath. Never increase it above 30 minutes as this allows the toddler to get a 'second wind'.
- A toddler who is not quite ready to sleep after the ritual can be allowed to listen to a nursery rhyme or story tape. This can be a great help in teaching him how to get off to sleep by himself.
- Just as feeding or rocking a baby to sleep can cause problems, so can reading or cuddling a toddler to sleep.

If, despite following all the above guidelines, your toddler contin-ues to fight sleep at 7–7.30pm, then you may have to incorporate the crying down or controlled crying methods as described on pages 66–69.

Sarah: aged 23 months

Sarah had never slept well as a baby, and did not sleep properly through the night until she was sleep trained at 18 months. After 18 months of waking up two and three times a night, her mother was delighted to settle for Sarah going to bed around 9pm, and waking at 6–7am. She also took a nap of two hours in the middle of the day, which helped her mother cope with her difficult behav-iour between 6.30pm and 9pm after which she would fall asleep exhausted in the cot drinking her bottle of formula. This pattern continued until her brother was born five months later.

Simon weighed over 10lb at birth, and by four weeks had out-grown the small Moses basket he had been sleeping in. Because Sarah had occasionally slept in a bed at her grandmother's house, the obvious decision was to put Sarah in the big bed and give Simon the cot.

The first night Sarah was so excited about going into her big bed that it took her mother slightly longer to settle her to sleep. Sarah would keep getting in and out of the bed, demanding yet another story to be read. She eventually fell asleep in her mother's arms at around 9.40pm, only to wake screaming at around mid-night. Sarah's mother had to spend another hour lying on the bed with her before she fell asleep. She awoke twice more in the night and each time it took nearly an hour to settle her. The following evening Sarah took even longer to settle, falling asleep at 10.15pm, and like the previous night woke up three times. During the following week a pattern quickly emerged of Sarah not settling to sleep until nearly 11pm, and waking two or three times in the night.

She would only fall asleep if her mother read or sang to her which could take anything up to 2 hours.

When her mother rang me for help it was clear that putting Sarah in the big bed was a major contribution to Sarah's sleeping problems. I suggested that she should put Sarah back in her cot. Fortunately, a friend had a spare cot that could be borrowed for Simon, and Sarah was transferred back to her old cot. The number of night wakings was immediately reduced, and when she did wake, her mother managed to settle her back to sleep quickly. However, settling Sarah at bedtime continued to be a problem. Her mother would start settling her at 9pm, but it was usually between 10pm and 11pm before she would fall asleep. I believe that the reason for this was that, like a baby who associates falling asleep with being fed or rocked, Sarah associated falling asleep with being read or sung to.

When Sarah was transferred to the bed and resisted sleep, the already late bedtime meant she got very overtired and fought sleep even more. Therefore, the time her mother spent reading and singing began to get longer and longer. I advised her mother gradually to bring Sarah's bedtime forward by 30 minutes every three nights until it was 7.30pm, and that she should spend no more than 20 minutes singing and reading to Sarah. Because Sarah had been used to a late bedtime for such a long time, I suggested that her mother should play a tape of gentle nursery rhymes for 40 minutes after leaving the room. She should tell Sarah that she was going to have a bath and would come back for one final 'night-night' when the tape was finished. If Sarah shouted out she was to say that she was in the bath and would come soon. By the time the tape was finished Sarah was always fast asleep. Within two weeks the length of time the tape was played was reduced to 20 minutes, and Sarah was sleeping from 7.30pm–7am.

Each morning Sarah's mother would tell her that she had gone in after the bath and given her a big night-night kiss.

Waking in the night

Sometimes a toddler who has slept well throughout the first year can suddenly begin to wake up in the night during the second year. Many parents assume that these wakings are caused by nightmares. However, the majority of childcare experts who have studied children's sleep patterns would disagree with this diagnosis. Most believe that nightmares for children under two years of age are very rare. Dr Brian Symon explains that the brain of a child of this age is not yet able to process information in such a complex way as to cause nightmares. He believes that parents should look for other reasons that may be causing their toddler to wake up.

Listed below are the most common causes that I have found for a toddler waking in the night and some suggestions for dealing with these wakings.

Routine

During the second year toddlers become more mobile and usually begin to attend more activities that can leave them physically and mentally exhausted. Those who do not have a regular day-time nap or a specific bedtime are more prone to overtiredness, which itself can result in night-time wakings. It is essential to establish a regular time for the day-time nap and for bedtime and then to stick to it.

Dummy

A toddler who has been allowed to have a dummy in bed can wake up several times a night if he loses the dummy. The only way to deal with this problem is to get rid of the dummy altogether and use the controlled crying method described on page 67.

New baby

The arrival of a new baby can sometimes cause a toddler to wake in the night. Try to structure a routine so that you manage to give him some undivided attention during the day When you attend to him in the night keep the reassurances short and simple and do not get involved in long discussions. A toddler who is feeling neglected during the day will try to make up for the attention which he feels he is missing in the night.

Anxiety

The arrival of a new baby, a house move, starting nursery or separation anxiety when a mother returns to work can cause a toddler to be anxious and start waking in the night. Sometimes buying a special cuddly toy that stays in the cot at all times can help make the toddler feel more secure. Special attention should be given to the toddler during the day to help overcome his feelings of anxiety.

Stories and videos

During the latter part of the second year a toddler's imagination becomes more active, and choosing the wrong bedtime stories or videos can overstimulate or upset some toddlers. Try to avoid excessive video watching prior to bedtime and choose simple stories that do not fuel his imagination.

Tantrums

Tears before bedtime can often result in the toddler waking in the night. Tantrums that end in tears are usually caused by overexcitement, overstimulation or confrontation. It is essential that bedtime rituals are kept calm and consistent.

The big bed

In my experience, transferring the toddler to a big bed before he is ready can be a major cause of night-time waking. Many parents make this transfer between 18 months and two years of age, often prompted by the fact a new baby is on the way and the cot will be needed. Other parents will listen to the advice of friends who say that their toddler sleeps much better now he is in a bed. To me this implies that their toddler's sleeping habits were probably not very good in the first place!

   The majority of my clients leave their toddlers in a cot until they are nearer three years of age. The fact that all of these toddlers are still sleeping in a sleeping bag, the possibility of them trying to climb out of the cot never arises. If a cot is needed for a second baby, many parents choose to buy a second cot, or a cot bed into which the toddler can be transferred before the new baby arrives. This can eventually be used as a first bed for the second baby. If you have already transferred your toddler to a bed and he is getting up several times a night, see Andrea's problem below and how it was dealt with.

Before transferring your toddler to a bed consider the following points.

- A toddler who is transferred to a bed too early is more likely to wake up early or get up in the night. He is inclined to get more upset than an older child when parents try to resettle him back to sleep in his own bed, and often ends up sleeping in his parents' bed.
- The arrival of a new baby often prompts the toddler to get out of bed, if he hears the baby crying in the night. He quickly learns to demand the same attention as the baby in the night – feeds and a cuddle.
- A toddler who is potty trained and sleeping in a bed will be more likely to take his nappy off in the night, even if he is not able to get through the night without a nappy.
- Once the nappy is abandoned at night, a potty and a night light usually have to be put in the toddler's room. In my experience, toddlers under three years of age who are sleeping in a bed, and who need to have a night light are much more likely to wake in the night and be difficult to settle back to sleep.

Andrea: aged 20 months

Andrea was 20 months when her parents transferred her into a bed, so they could give her cot to her brother David, aged five months. It was a total disaster, which resulted in Andrea waking and crying and wandering out of her room several times a night. When her mother tried shutting the door Andrea became absolutely hysterical. After a week of virtually no sleep, they transferred David to a travel cot and put Andrea back in her cot. She continued to cry hysterically until she was sick. Sometimes she would do this twice in succession. Eventually in desperation her parents decided to move the cot back to David's room and put Andrea back in her bed, with the door shut. She never stayed in bed. She would spend hours crying hysterically, and pounding her fists on the door. Andrea sounded so petrified, that her mother quickly gave up on the idea and ended up taking Andrea into her own bed. She would not go to bed until her parents did and con-

tinued to wake up crying and would wander out of the room several times a night. Andrea's lack of sleep started to affect her behaviour at nursery. She was tired and groggy and did not join in with the other children.

Her mother also became tired and so low spirited that she started to let David's routine slip. As a means of settling him back to sleep once he had been woken by Andrea's constant crying, she resorted to giving David a bottle. The whole situation was a nightmare, that was repeated night after night.

After several weeks of sleep deprivation, the parents rang me to see if I could help get both the children's sleeping and feeding sorted out. I agreed to help on the condition that they went out and bought another cot. I firmly believed that Andrea was far too young to sleep in a bed.

On the first night that Andrea was to go back in her cot I advised the parents to stick to the same bedtime – of around midnight. She immediately started trembling and crying when she was put in to it. Following my advice, her mother sat on a chair right next to the cot, cuddling and reassuring Andrea, and saying 'Mummy's here, lie down and go to sleep'. It was an hour before Andrea calmed down and showed signs of sleepiness. Her mother spent a further 15 minutes sitting beside the cot before saying 'night-night'. She gave Andrea one last cuddle before leaving the room. Andrea immediately started crying. This went on for 15 minutes and then she was violently sick. Following my advice, Andrea was changed and comforted, without being lifted out of the cot. Her mother then sat right next to the cot again, and continued the settling pattern as before. Andrea was now very tired, but fighting sleep. Eventually, after 40 minutes, she lay down and closed her eyes for short spells. Her mother, gradually started to edge her chair further and further away from the cot, but when she got near to the door Andrea stood up and started crying again. By this time, her mother was so exhausted that she decided that she would to have to leave Andrea to cry. She gave her one last cuddle and told her to 'Lie down and go to sleep'. Andrea cried for one hour before falling asleep.

Over the next three nights Andrea's bedtime was gradually brought forward, and the amount of time her mother spent settling her was reduced. She was never lifted out of the cot, no matter how hard she screamed. Her mother would stroke her *forehead and keep repeating the same phrase: 'Lie down and go to sleep'. The number of times Andrea awoke and the amount of time she cried lessened each night. By the fourth night Andrea's bedtime had been brought forward to 8.30pm and she slept solidly for 11 hours.*

During those five days we also solved the problem of Andrea's refusal to eat. She was still drinking milk from a bottle, at an average of two and a half pints a day – approximately 1,500 ml! This is an excessive amount of milk and is the reason why Andrea constantly refused to eat her meals. Some days she would only eat a slice or two of bread or a yoghurt. During those five days we eliminated all the bottles of milk from Andrea's diet. She would drink juice from a cup, but refused to drink milk from a cup. However, this immediately brought about a huge increase in Andrea's appetite and she would take milk on her cereal, in sauces or puddings. I advised her mother to include lots of calcium rich foods in Andrea's diet, to ensure she received her necessary daily intake of calcium.

NB: The current advice given by the Department of Health is that children over one year should not be given milk to drink from a bottle, as it reduces their appetite for other foods. A child over one year of age needs a minimum of 350ml (11½oz) of milk a day, inclusive of milk used in food.

5
Potty training

'At what age should I start to potty train?' and 'How long will it take?' are questions I am frequently asked by parents. While all children are different, in my experience of working with hundreds of mothers and children, the majority are ready to be trained somewhere between the ages of 18 and 24 months. Before 18 months, very few children's muscles are developed enough for the bladder control necessary for potty training. While we have all heard the stories from our mothers, aunties and grandmas, how in their day the baby was potty trained by the age of one year, the reality is that it was really the mother who was trained and not the baby. By sitting the baby on the potty at frequent times during the day she would, more often than not, catch the urine or the bowel movement. While this obviously saved her the laborious task of washing and sterilising the terry nappies used in those days, the baby could not be called potty trained in the true sense.

A toddler who is truly potty trained will recognise when he needs to pass urine or have a bowel movement and be capable of going to his potty, pulling down his own pants, and using the potty before pulling his pants up again.

When to start

Once your toddler reaches 18 months there are signs to watch out for that indicate he may be ready for potty training. However, I should point out that the success of potty-training quickly will not only depend on your toddler being ready, but also on you being ready. All too often I hear horror stories of how potty training was a nightmare and took ages, the conclusion being that the child wasn't ready. In reality it was very often the parents who weren't ready. Even if your toddler is showing most of the signs listed below it would be inadvisable to begin training unless you have the time to devote yourself to the task 100 per cent. It is not something to undertake if you are about to move house, have just had a baby, or your toddler is just getting over an illness.

To train your toddler quickly and successfully, it is very important that not only are you in a relaxed state of mind, but also that any older or younger siblings are happy and in a good enough routine to allow 100 per cent concentration and the extra time needed if you want to achieve this.

Provided you are feeling in a positive frame of mind, the time is right for the rest of the family, and your toddler is showing all of the signs listed below, you should manage to train him successfully within one week.

These are the important signs that will indicate if your toddler is ready to potty train.

- He is over 18 months of age and his nappy is frequently dry when you get him up from his lunch-time nap. A dry nappy a couple of hours after his last nappy change would also be an indication that he is getting some bladder control.
- He shows signs of awareness when doing a poo; ie he goes very quiet and squeezes his legs together, or points to his nappy and says 'poo' or 'pee pee' when he has done one.
- He can understand and follow simple instructions; ie 'go and fetch your red ball' or 'put your toy in the box'.
- He is eager to participate in taking off his own clothes; ie shoes, socks and shorts, and understands what pulling his shorts up and down mean.
- He has the ability to sit still and occupy himself or concentrate for 5–10 minutes with a toy or a book.

Things needed for potty training

Before you begin to think of preparing your child for potty training make sure that you have all the right equipment.

Two potties

It is essential to have two potties, one for upstairs and one for downstairs, as it saves having to transfer them up and down stairs. Remember that during the early stages of training it is often a case of getting the potty to the child, rather than the child to the potty. They should be of a simple, sturdy design with a wide brim and a splash guard at the front. They should also have an extra-wide base so that the potty stays on the floor when your child stands up. Avoid fancy or complicated designs with lids at this stage.

Child's loo seat

This is a specially designed seat that fits inside the loo seat. Choose one that is well padded, and has handles at each side which the child can hold onto to keep himself steady.

Ten pairs of pants

It is important to buy pants a couple of sizes bigger, making it easier for your child to pull them up and down by himself. This also allows for shrinkage due to constant washing and drying.

Selection of story books, cassette tapes and videos

Buy a selection of short story books and nursery rhyme tapes so he is less likely to become bored while on the potty. Video some suitable children's programmes, which can be used as a last resort if he becomes stubborn about using the potty.

Star chart

Design a brightly coloured star chart with his name on it, and buy lots of different coloured stars in assorted sizes. When he has successfully used the potty several times in a row, give him an extra big star for being so clever.

Face cloths

It is easier for a small child to dry his hands himself on a small face cloth than on a towel. Choose several decorated with his favourite cartoon characters to encourage hand washing after using the potty.

Booster step

This is a small step for your child to stand on. It enables him to reach the basin more easily when washing his hands, and eventually it helps him to reach the loo.

Clothing

For the first few days of potty training it is better for you to dress your child in a very short tee shirt that does not need to be pulled up above the pants. However, once the training is under way and going well make sure you dress him in clothes that he finds quick and easy to handle when he uses the potty. For example, vests that fasten between the legs should be changed to ordinary ones, also avoid dungarees and trousers with lots of buttons and belts. Until he is trained it is better to go for simple shorts or tracksuit type bottoms with a simple tee shirt or sweat shirt.

Preparation for training: Stage one

If your toddler is nearing 18 months there are many things that you can do to help prepare him for potty training. As all children of this age love to role play, the first step is to take him to the bathroom with you as often as possible. At this stage do not remove his nappy but do encourage him to sit on his potty and watch you as you demonstrate and describe what you are doing. This will go a long way towards teaching your child in advance what will eventually be expected of him. The important thing at this stage is that he learns to sit still on the potty while you explain what you are doing using clear simple language. The following example illustrates the main points you want to get across to your child.

- 'Mummy needs to go and do a pee pee'
  Helpful action: take his hand and lead him to the bathroom.
- 'Mummy does pee pee in the loo'
  Helpful action: show him the loo, pointing where the pee pee goes.
- 'Mummy is pulling down her pants'
  Helpful action: demonstrate how you pull your pants down.
- 'Mummy is going to sit down on the loo and do pee pee, and James can sit on his potty'
  Helpful action: applaud when he sits on his potty and praise him by saying: 'James is such a clever boy sitting so still on his potty'
- 'Mummy has finished pee pee and she's going to pull up her nice dry pants'
  Helpful action: demonstrate how you pull your pants up.

Finally, when you wash your hands encourage him to join in, washing and drying his own hands at the same time as you are doing yours. Place a lot of emphasis on the words 'wet' and 'dry', demonstrating how his hands become wet with water when washed, then dry when wiped with the towel. Occasionally, it is a good idea deliberately to wet the hand towel; allow him to feel the wet towel as you explain how much nicer it is to dry his hands on a clean dry towel. He should then be allowed to choose between the wet and the dry towel, for drying hands. This will help him to understand the difference between wet and dry.

When he shows signs of trying to copy you and participate in the above procedures, provided he is also showing some of the other signs of readiness for potty training, he should be encouraged to sit on his potty without his nappy while you prepare the bath. A time limit of 5–10 minutes is long enough and if he manages to do anything in the potty remember to give lots of praise. When praising your child it is important that he understands why you are pleased with him. For example it is better to say how clever he is at sitting on his potty, or how clever he is at peeing in his potty than to say what a good boy he is, as he may start to think he is bad if he doesn't manage to make it to the potty.

Once he has been happy to sit on the potty at bath time, you should try sitting him on it after breakfast and when you get him up from his nap. If he has been happy sitting on his potty at the above times for at least a week, you can seriously consider putting him in pants and training him to use the potty during the day. However, as I keep stressing, the success of the potty training will depend not only on your child being ready, but also on you being ready.

Clean before dry

Many children are clean before they are dry, as is easier for them to control their bowels than their bladders. If your child does a poo around the the same time every day, it is worthwhile sitting him on the potty at that time, as well as the times mentioned above. It can be a bit hit and miss at this stage: sometimes a child will do a poo in the potty, other times he will do it the minute he puts his nappy on. If this happens do not make a fuss, simply change his nappy and tell him that the next time he needs a poo he should try to do it in his potty. The important thing is not to show disapproval or to scold the child if he doesn't manage to poo in the potty every time. Encouragement and gentle reassurance will, in the long term, get better results.

How to train: Stage two

If you have spent a minimum of two weeks following the procedures laid out in the preparation section, and also your child shows most of the signs of readiness listed earlier you should be able to train your child successfully in one week. It is very important to choose a week that is fairly free of activities, especially for the first couple of days, so explain to family and friends that you are potty training and will be unavailable for telephone calls and visits during the day time. If you have other children it is probably better to start at the weekend, when your husband can help out.

Your toddler will need your constant attention and encouragement during the first couple of days, otherwise he will very quickly lose interest.

Day one

On the first day of training, once he has had his breakfast he should be put straight into his 'special big boy pants'. If you have followed the steps listed in the preparation stage he will already have some idea of what is he is expected to do, so keep explanations and instructions as clear and simple as possible. Explain simply that he is a big boy now and can wear pants like Mummy and Daddy, and that he can use his potty when he needs to do a pee pee or poo. Also continue taking him with you to to the bathroom and explaining what you are doing. Suggest he sits on his potty at the same time so that you can both do a pee pee.

During the first couple of days he will need frequent reminders to sit on the potty, therefore it is better to try and contain the training to one room. If you have to move between two rooms, make sure that you are prepared and have a selection of books already in each room. It is very important that should you need to go to the other room for even a few minutes, you take the toddler and the potty.

He should be encouraged to sit on the potty every 15 minutes from when he last finished, ideally for a period of 5–10 minutes each time. Some children are happy to sit longer and others get bored very quickly. If your child is one of the latter, encourage him to look at a book or sing along to his cassette tape. Once he has successfully used the potty several times, the length of time between reminders can be gradually extended. The length of time it takes for a child to use the potty several times successfully, varies from child to child. Some of the children I have trained pee regularly in the potty within a couple of hours, but with others it can take several hours. Do not despair if your child wets his pants several times before he manages to do it in the potty. Once he does manage to pee in it a couple of times in a row, he will be so proud of himself that he will be very keen to keep showing you his new skill.

The important thing is not to make a big fuss or show displeasure when he does have an accident. Change his pants and continue to be enthusiastic about his big boy pants and how clever he is at sitting on his potty. When he is successful at using the potty, tell him how clever he is at peeing in the potty and how happy and proud Daddy will be. Lots of praise, hugs and applause along with the use of a star chart is the most effective way of encouraging him to continue using the potty. All children respond better to encouragement and praise than to criticism, and also the star chart will be a visible reminder of how clever he is at using the potty.

I have found it very useful to keep a second chart detailing the progress of potty training. It is a great help to see a pattern emerging of how often he needs to urinate, and whether successful use of the potty was self-motivated or not.

Draw a simple chart like the one on page 118, and record the time he urinates and tick the appropriate column. In the potty column, use one tick when he urinates in the potty after being instructed by you, and two ticks when he urinates in the potty of his own accord.

By the end of the first day, there should be more ticks in the potty column than in the accident column. If your child has no ticks in the potty column it is clear that, for whatever reason, he is not ready and it would be better to go back to the preparation stage for a further week or two.

However, if your child has shown all the signs of readiness and you have followed all the preparation instructions laid out in Stage one, he will probably have at least two or three ticks in the potty column.

POTTY PROGRESS CHART			
Time	*Potty*	*Accident*	*Comments*

At the end of the first day regardless of how successful he was at using his potty, it is important to tell your child how proud you are of him for being so clever at using his potty. No reference should be made to any accidents that have occurred during the day. Also it helps to reinforce the idea of wearing pants if you get him to choose the ones he will wear the following day.

To help avoid boredom setting in during the second day of training, try to arrange for one of his friends to come round for a short play date. This can be used as a further encouragement to your child; ie 'Tommy will be so excited to see you in your big boy pants when he visits tomorrow'. It is even better if the friend is potty trained or being potty trained.

Day two

By the second day of training, your chart should begin to show a pattern of more regular intervals between the times your child needs to pass urine. This pattern will serve as a guide as to how often you need to remind him, and how often he is using the potty of his own accord. Obviously the aim is that he needs fewer and fewer reminders from you and there are fewer accidents. For this to happen it is important that the potty is still kept within full view and within easy reach.

As the day progesses you should gradually go from reminding him to sit on the potty, to asking him if he needs to use the potty. It is important for his mental and physical awareness that you start to allow him some of the responsibility of deciding when he needs to use the potty, even if it means occasional accidents. Accidents will be more likely to happen if your child is playing and forgets or if he gets excited.

Day three

By the third day, a definite pattern should have emerged of how often he needs to use the potty. The progress chart should be of help when planning the best time for your first outing. Ideally, it should be a short visit to one of his friends who lives close by. Before leaving the house your toddler should be encouraged to use the potty so as to avoid any accidents on the journey. Do not be tempted to put him back into a nappy or disposable pull-up trainer pants on outings as this will only give confusing signals, and is one of the main reasons why potty training can take so long.

Consistency is of the utmost importance if you want to potty train quickly and successfully. Dress your toddler in pants at all times during the day – nappies are for sleep times only. While there may be a few accidents during the first few days, these mishaps will actually help your child to become more aware of his need to urinate, and the difference between wet and dry. It is best not to make a fuss or scold your toddler if he has an accident, simply remind him what the potty is for.

In the early days it is advisable to take a couple of spare changes of clothes and pants on outings and a plastic bag to put them in if they get wet. Until your toddler gets used to using the lavatory you will also need to take his potty. Although I have never used one for a toddler, there are special portable potties now available for travelling.

Until your toddler is properly trained it is advisable to take precautions when travelling in the car, or using the buggy. I would advise buying a thin cushion pad and covering it with a polythene bag. This can then be covered with a removable, washable, decorative cover. It can be your child's special cushion and be used in the buggy, car seat or when visiting friends, and is safer than just placing a plastic bag on the seat. I have found that when a plastic bag is placed on a seat, the child often sees it as a safety net and is less inclined to mention that he needs to pee. He is unaware that his cushion has a plastic cover, and because it is his special cushion he will more likely want to keep it dry.

Days four to seven

By the fourth day, the majority of toddlers are regularly using their potty without prompting, with just the occasional accident occurring. Over the next few days the potty should gradually be moved nearer and nearer to the bathroom. Once your toddler shows signs that he can control his bladder long enough to get to the bathroom, it should remain there permanently. If a couple of hours have gone by without using the potty, and he seems particularly engrossed in something, it would be a good idea to remind him where the potty is.

By the end of the first week, the majority of toddlers are dry most of the time, with only the occasional accident. To ensure continued success it is important that you never put your toddler back in nappies apart from sleep times. This only confuses the toddler and is one of the main reasons potty training can become a problem and take many months to crack.

Sleep times

I would continue to put a toddler in nappies during his day-time sleep until his nappy has been consistently dry for at least two weeks when he gets up. After that I would feel confident it was safe to abandon it. For the night-time sleep, I would continue with nappies for several months. It is my experience that very few children are capable of going through the night before the age of three years, and with boys it may be even later.

I have found that parents who push night-time training before this age often end up with other problems. One major one is that once the nappy is abandoned it is usually necessary either to install a night light or leave the door slightly ajar. With toddlers under three years the temptation to start running around in the middle of the night is often too hard to resist, especially if they know Mummy is attending to a younger sibling. With a child over three years who is consistently dry and clean, I would explain that he no longer needs to wear a nappy at night, and make sure that he goes on the potty just before he gets into bed. Once your child stops wearing a nappy at night it is important to make sure that the last drink is given at least an hour before bedtime.

Beatrice: aged twenty-seven months

Beatrice was just over two years old when her mother started potty training her and she was both clean and dry by the end of the first week. During the weeks that followed she rarely had any accidents and her nappy was dry most mornings. When she reached 26 months her mother was confident that she was ready to abandon the night-time nappy. Beatrice continued to stay dry both during the day and at night for a further two weeks. Then suddenly one morning at around 5am Beatrice's parents were woken up by hysterical screaming. Beatrice, who had always slept soundly from 7pm–7am, was inconsolable. It was clear that she wasn't ill, but her parents could not fathom out what had caused the waking. It was not until 20 minutes later, when she had eventually calmed down, that she asked for her potty. At this stage her parents did not see the connection of her wanting to use the potty with the waking, as she had been dry at night for so many weeks.

However, the next night the same thing happened again and they then decided to put her potty in the room. They placed it next to a small plug-in night light, and explained to her that if she woke in the night and needed to wee, her potty was right beside her.

That night Beatrice did not settle well at 7pm. She kept getting out of bed, running around the room opening drawers and cupboards, and shouting for her parents. After many return visits by her parents to Beatrice's room and several sittings on the potty, she eventually settled to sleep at 9pm.

She continued to be difficult to settle at night and after a couple of weeks her parents began to experience problems in settling her for the day-time nap. The late bedtime and shorter lunch-time nap resulted in her becoming overtired, irritable and very fretful during the day. Realising that they now had a serious sleep problem on their hands, they contacted me for help.

Because Beatrice was no longer in her sleeping bag and cot, putting a nappy back on and removing the night light was not an option that could be used to solve this problem. I therefore suggested that they try the method used for a late bedtime problem (see page 103) along with the advice for dealing with a toddler who keeps getting out of bed (see page 108).

After two weeks Beatrice was settling well at night, at nap time, and also after using the potty in the night. I believe that Beatrice's problem was definitely caused by her parents taking her out of night-time nappies too early, which meant installing a potty and a night light in her room.

Very few children under three years of age have enough bladder control to sleep a 12 hour night. Hence my advice that parents of toddlers under three years who wish to avoid sleep problems, should think seriously before abandoning the sleeping bag and cot, which would also restrict a toddler who attempts to take his nappy off.

Bedwetting

It is fairly common for young children to have an occasional accident at night. However, it can be a real problem if the bedwetting becomes a regular occurrence. The broken nights' sleep and changing wet sheets can be exhausting for parents and lead to the child feeling anxious and guilty. If your child has been dry for many weeks and suddenly starts wetting the bed, a visit to the doctor should be considered to rule out the possibility of an urinary infection. Many experts suggest that a relapse may also be caused by emotional problems, but in my experience this is rarely the case. The majority of the parents I have worked with believe that excessive amounts of fluid prior to bedtime can be a major cause of bedwetting, therefore they allow no drinks after 6pm.

With a child under four years who has only been dry for a few weeks, and then starts to wet the bed regularly, it is probably because he isn't quite ready to last through the night. It may be preferable to put him back in nappies for a short while, to avoid bedwetting becoming an issue.

If your child is over four years of age and, despite restricting fluids, you are getting a wet bed every morning, it may be worthwhile lifting him and putting him on the potty at your bedtime.

Lifting at 10pm

Years ago, childcare experts advised parents to lift their baby at 10pm, and put him on the potty to pass urine. These experts believed that the age at which a child gains bladder control at night, depends largely on the mother's skill in training him in infancy.

The childcare manuals written in the 1930s and 1940s stressed that lifting should be a habit that is formed in infancy. Mothers were advised that regularly lifting the child every night until he was four years old was key to teaching him how to stay dry throughout the night. If their laziness prevented them from doing this, they would create a habit difficult to cure; a child who got used to waking up with a wet nappy would quickly begin to believe that it was normal.

While many parents do still lift their children at their bedtime, the majority of childcare experts today are against this practice. They believe that this approach only conditions the child to pass urine at certain times. I would tend to agree with this, and would only consider lifting a child if he was over four years of age, and despite monitoring fluids in the evening, the bed was wet every morning.

A nanny friend and I successfully used the lifting approach as a last resort when working in the Middle East with a family of serious bedwetters. The six children from 4–14 years were taken very sleepily at different times to the loo in the late late evening. Occasionally, one or the other would wake up wet, but much to the relief of the laundry staff, most mornings the beds were dry.

If you decide to try this approach it is important that the child is kept sleepy and not stimulated. The lights should be kept very dim, and talking, if any, kept to the minimum. Children under three years could be put on the potty, instead of being taken to the bathroom. Some experts claim that varying the time of lifting will help reduce the possibility of conditioning the child's need to urinate at the same time every night.

If you find that lifting your child is working, it is worthwhile using a star chart. On the mornings when the bed is dry he gets a star; three stars and he gets a special treat – perhaps an ice-cream.

If the bedwetting improves, I would advise telling your child that he is a big boy now and doesn't need lifting any more in the night. Suggest to him that if he does wake in the night and needs a pee he should call for you to come and help him. Although it will mean you getting up in the night for a short while, I usually find that as his confidence increases, the child will be persuaded to use the potty by himself.

Again I have found that, if used properly, the star chart is very effective during these various stages.

The stubborn child

Occasionally, I have a child who refuses to go on the potty, but if he is under 2½ years I would not force the issue. However, with a child nearer three years of age who refuses to sit on the potty I would probably resort to bribery. I know the majority of experts frown upon this advice, but sometimes, especially with a very stubborn child, it is the only way.

While a child over three years may not show all the signs necessary for potty training, he is usually capable of being trained. I would skip the preparation stage and go straight into potty training and use a star chart. I would explain that every time he does a pee in the potty he would get a star – and for every star he would get a treat. The treat can be a raisin or a very small sweet like a smartie. Believe me it does work, provided of course the child receives no other treats throughout the day. Within two days I find the child is regularly asking for the potty, then the star, followed by the treat. Once I see a regular pattern emerge I would explain to the child that I had run out of the treats.

I would suggest that the next three pees in the potty would deserve a trip to the shop for a special ice-cream. By using delaying tactics of a bigger treat for more pees in the potty, I would eventually arrive at a stage where the child uses the potty throughout the day, and ends up with only one treat in the evening.

Hygiene

During the early stages of potty training you will need to wipe your toddler's bottom, and help him wash and dry his hands. By the time they get to three years, most children are becoming more independent and insist on doing these things for themselves. It is important to help them practise how to wipe their bottoms properly (girls from front to back) and how to wash their hands thoroughly. The use of novelty soaps and hand towels with cartoons on them can help make hand washing and drying more fun. It essential to teach your child the importance of proper hygiene.

Regression

All toddlers and children will continue to have the occasional accident once they are potty trained. The important thing is to stay calm and consistent, and not be tempted to put him back into nappies if you have a bad couple of days. Occasionally, a toddler or child who has been dry for many months may regress completely. This often happens around the time when a new brother or sister arrives, when he starts playgroup or there is a similar emotional upheaval. If your child suddenly regresses and appears to be more withdrawn or is more demanding and displaying unusual aggressive behaviour, the regression is probably psychological. If his behaviour is normal it may be worth a visit to the doctor to rule out the possibility of a urine infection.

Whatever has caused the regression I would not advise going back to nappies. Although it may mean many wet pants for a short spell, being patient, consistent and encouraging will eventually get your child back on track. It is also worthwhile doing a progress chart for a couple of days again, to establish how often the accidents are happening. (See page 118.) A pattern usually emerges of how often he has an accident, and this will enable you to remind him to use the potty at these regular intervals. If he is reluctant to use the potty, take him with you when you need to go to the loo yourself. Making a game of using the loo at the same time will often encourage him to go on the potty, while you are using the loo. Obviously this plan is more likely to be successful if done at roughly the times you think he may need to pee.

Reintroducing a line on his star chart for successful use of the potty can also be an incentive.

Your questions answered

Q My son is only 16 months old and showing no awareness when he does a wee or a poo, but my mother keeps nagging me to start training. Do you think he is ready?

A • Very few children have the muscle control required for potty training before the age of 18 months and the majority are not ready until nearer the age of two years.

- His nappy should sometimes be dry when you get him up from his longest nap, or dry a couple of hours after his last nappy change.
- A child must understand and be capable of following simple instructions; ie 'Bring me your shoes', or 'Sit here until Mummy gets your jacket'.
- He should also be content to sit by himself and play with his toys or look at a simple book for at least ten minutes.
- He should be capable of taking off his socks and shoes, and attempting to pull down his shorts or trousers.

Q My 18-month-old points to her nappy when she does a poo, but shows none of the other signs. Should I attempt to potty train her?

A • It is unwise to start potty training until the child is clearly showing nearly all the signs. But, you can begin to prepare her for potty training by doing the following:
- Buy the potty and leave it in the bathroom, explain what it is for and encourage her to sit on it for a few minutes before she gets in the bath. Under no circumstances force the issue at this stage – allow her to take the lead.
- Take her to the bathroom when you go and explain what you are doing, but do not ask her if she wants to use her potty. Let her take the lead, she will very quickly start to copy you and sit on her potty.
- Start encouraging her to pull down and pull up her shorts by herself. Give lots of praise when she manages to do it.
- When she is playing with slightly older children, ask them if they mind her watching how clever they are at going on the potty or loo. Obviously, if the other children are not keen to perform, do not force the issue.
- At bath time and when she washes her hands, put lots of emphasis on the difference between the words 'wet' and 'dry'. Face cloths are a great way to demonstrate this. After a while ask her to show you the wet one, then the dry one.

Q We are going on holiday soon. My husband reckons that it would be a good time to begin training our toddler, as he could assist by helping with our young baby.

A • I would not advise potty training on holiday. A holiday normally is a time for lots of fun and activities. It would be unfair to expect the child to give potty training the concentration it requires.

• During the first couple of days of potty training it is much better if there are as few people around as possible, thus avoiding too many distractions.

• If you have a young baby, try to start training at the weekend so your husband can take care of the baby, allowing you to concentrate on the training. Make sure your husband has done a trial run of caring for the baby before you actually start the potty training. The fewer interruptions when you are training the better.

Q **What should I dress my child in during the potty training period?**

A • During the first two to three days when in the house it will be easier if you dress him in a very short tee shirt that does not need to be pulled up when he sits on the potty. He should also wear pants that are big enough to be easily pulled up and down.

• **When you have to take him out it is important that he continues to wear pants. Never go back to nappies once you've started, even if there are accidents. It's too confusing for the child, and the main reason why potty training fails.**

• Do not be tempted to use pull-up nappies as this will also confuse your child. Parents who use these on outings to avoid accidents take much longer to potty train their child, as the absorbency of the pull ups decreases the child's awareness of the difference between being wet and dry.

• Ensure that the outer garments are as simple as possible. Avoid lots of buttons, poppers or braces. Track suit bottoms or shorts and a loose short top are ideal.

Q **Should I reward my child with a sweet or a treat when he is successful in using the potty?**

A • It is better if you can avoid this type of bribery. A child under 2½ years will normally be happy with a star chart and lots of encouragement and praise.

- The only time I would compromise on this is if I am training an older child with a very stubborn streak. I would explain that once he had three stars on his chart he would get a small treat. Once he was using the potty regularly, I would tell him that when he has six stars on the chart he would get an ice-cream. This approach helps decrease the risk of the child only using the potty if he gets a reward.

Q My daughter, aged two years and eight months, has been dry for over six months, but she refuses to poo in her potty or the loo. She always waits until she has her nappy on and then does it.

A • This is a very common problem. In my experience it is more common among children who have irregular or hard bowel movements. It is worthwhile giving her more fruit to eat especially at breakfast time as this often helps to regulate the child's bowel movements. Once a regular time is established, line her potty with a nappy and encourage her to sit on it at that time. As a special treat let her watch her favourite video. Once she is regularly having a bowel movement, pretend to run out of nappies. With the help of a new book or video, she may be persuaded to use the potty without the nappy in it.

- If this fails it is best not to force the issue, just accept that she is going to poo in her nappy. The problem usually sorts itself out once the child is out of nappies altogether. However, I would not advise taking her out of nappies at sleep times too quickly, just to solve this problem. All too often I have seen children completely backtrack with loo training because of the parents' pressure.

- Also never attempt to break this habit by showing disgust at the dirty nappy, or scolding her. This sort of disapproval could lead to her becoming very worried and anxious, and withholding the poo altogether.

Leo: aged 30 months

Leo had been very enthusiastic about potty training and was completely dry by 25 months. Within a couple of weeks of being trained he was also happy to use the big loo. However, when it came to doing a poo he simply refused to use either the potty or the loo. No matter how desperate he was to open his bowels, he would hold on until he had his nappy on at his day-time nap or at bedtime. By the time I arrived to help care for Leo's new-born baby sister, opening his bowels had become a real problem. Sometimes he would go three or four days before eventually passing a very hard bowel motion in his nappy or pants. The discomfort of passing these hard bowel movements made Leo even more reluctant to sit on his potty or the loo.

While it is perfectly normal for some children to become dry long before they are clean, a problem like Leo's can quickly evolve if the refusal to poo in the potty or on the loo is handled wrongly.

Within days of my arrival it was clear that this is exactly what had happened to Leo. I observed that the nanny insisted that he sit on the loo several times a day and try to do a poo. She would talk a great deal about him being a big boy now, and how big boys don't do poos in their pants. He was constantly reminded of how clever his friends were for doing their poos in the potty, and how they would laugh at him for being such a baby. Each time he had done a poo in his pants he was reprimanded and told how smelly and disgusting it was.

Although the nanny meant well, it was clear that her obsession with getting Leo to be clean was making him very anxious and causing him to hold back on his bowel movements. We must remember that when young babies are in nappies, they may never actually have seen their poo. Hence, when it is eventually shown to them and they are told how revolting it is (usually both at the same time) this can be a personal afront to them and can leave them with an association that is psychologically disturbing. Persistent retention of bowel movements can result in the child becoming very constipated, which in turn results in a great deal of pain when he does eventually have a bowel movement.

I suggested to the nanny and to Leo's parents that they should stop pressurising him to do a poo on the loo or potty. During the following week no comment whatsoever should be made when he filled his pants or nappy, and it was very important that words like 'smelly' and 'disgusting' were not used. I also advised them to keep increasing his intake of fruit and fluids until he was no longer constipated, and until he was having a bowel movement every day.

Once he was having a bowel movement each day they could then comment on how clever he was and how much easier it would be to do the nice soft poo on the loo. It was essential that no other references were made to his bowel movements. Although it took nearly three weeks, Leo eventually went to the loo of his own accord and passed a bowel movement.

The parents then introduced a column on his star chart and for every six stars in the potty column he was allowed a special treat. The parents continued to keep a very close watch on his diet, ensuring that it contained enough fruit, vegetables and fluid to help avoid constipation. Leo continues to use the big loo and takes much pride in the size and colour of his poos!

Q When should I start to get my daughter to use the loo instead of the potty?

A • Once she has developed enough bladder control to reach her potty in the bathroom, she should be encouraged to use the big loo. It is best to insert a specially designed child's loo seat that fits securely inside the big seat. The ones that are padded appear to be more popular with young children, and some even come with handles for them to hold on to.

• The loo can seem very big and frightening to a toddler. To avoid long-term problems in using the loo it is important that you not only hold her around her waist, but also that you kneel down, so that you are face-to-face. Proper eye contact will help reassure her that nothing awful is going to happen.

• Once you feel your toddler is confident about sitting on the big loo, hold her with only one hand. As her confidence increases, continue to get down to her level so she doesn't feel intimidated or alone, but encourage her to sit, while supporting herself. These few very simple measures will ensure that she quickly builds up her confidence to sit on the seat unaided.

Q My son is two and a half years old and has been clean and dry for nearly three months, but still sits when he needs to wee. At what age will he be capable of standing up and weeing?

A • Many boys are nearer three years of age before they start to wee standing up. This is usually around the same time that they start nursery and see how other boys are doing it. All children love to copy, so encourage him to go to the loo with Daddy or other boys as much as possible.

- If he is still not quite tall enough to aim into the loo easily, he may need to stand on a small step. He may need to be held under the arms until he learns to balance confidently by himself.

- He may also need assistance in the early days in learning how high to hold his penis up, so he can aim into the loo. When he is finished teach him to shake his penis over the loo, to avoid drips on the carpet.

- If he is unsure or reluctant about standing up and weeing into the loo, try getting him to wee into a disposable plastic cup over the loo bowl. This trick seems to have worked with many of my little boys who have been hesitant about using the loo.

Q Once he is successfully potty trained how long do I wait before taking him out of nappies at sleep times?

A • Continue to use nappies at the lunch-time nap. If he is consistently dry when he gets up for at least two weeks, you could then abandon the nappies.

- For the night-time sleep I usually wait until the child is at least three years of age. If, on waking, his nappy is dry or only slightly damp for several weeks, you could then abandon the night-time nappy.

- If you find he then starts to wake up in the night needing his potty, at this age he should be capable of getting out of bed and using the potty by himself. Obviously, you would have to install a small, very dim night light.

- I have found that installing a night light with very young children can often lead to disturbed sleep and more night wakings, so try and avoid this until he is nearer three years.

Q Is it advisable to use a waterproof sheet once he is out of night-time nappies?

A • There are special waterproof pads that can go across the middle of the bed which can help when accidents occur.

- If your child is one of the few that does not like the feel of these pads, use a water-proof sheet on top of the mattress, then the fitted sheet, then a further pad and finally a further fitted sheet. This way if your child does have an accident in the night, it is just a case of whipping the first two layers away, and avoids having to remake the bed completely.

- Finally remember that your child should not have excessive drinks before bedtime. A cup of milk should be given no later than 6pm, and if he is still thirsty at bedtime offer a small amount of water.

Q **My three-year-old son manages to stay dry most nights and we are thinking of taking him out of night nappies. My mother has suggested we should lift him at our bedtime and put him on the potty to avoid a wet bed.**

A • Many parents believe that lifting their child to wee at bedtime encourages night training. Some experts believe that this practice only conditions the child to pass urine at certain times, and actually delays the child in learning night-time bladder control.

- I have found it is better to accept an occasional wet bed. The child then learns to control his bladder naturally, and to get up to use the potty when he needs to. However, if a child was over four years of age and regularly wetting the bed I would consider 'lifting' him.

- Before abandoning the night nappy, check the amount he is drinking at bedtime. If it is a huge amount, gradually cut back. Explain to him that he must have his big drink before 6pm, as he will only be allowed a small drink of water at bedtime.

- Once you are happy that he is not drinking an excessive amount at bedtime, explain he is a big boy now and no longer needs to wear a nappy during the night. Ensure that he goes on the potty just before he gets into bed.

- If you find you are getting the occasional accident, install a night light and leave a potty in his room. Explain that he should use the potty in the night when he needs to do a wee. Once he is older his door can be left slightly open so that he can make his way to the bathroom.

6

Habits: the good, the bad and the ugly

While much of this book focuses on establishing good feeding and sleeping habits for babies and toddlers, there are other good habits that can be learned from an early age. Teeth cleaning and hand washing are two that spring to mind. If introduced correctly and in a positive manner at a young age many battles can be avoided at a later date.

There are also some habits formed in the early days that are considered good at the time but at a later stage are looked upon as bad. For example, most mothers give a sigh of relief when their young baby eventually finds his thumb and many mothers actively encourage the habit by pushing the baby's thumb into his mouth. The mother believes thumb sucking will be an excellent source of comfort and a way for the baby to resettle himself to sleep should he wake in the night or very early morning. But if the child is still sucking his thumb three years down the line, it is a different story. The mother gets annoyed and often embarrassed if the child constantly has his thumb in his mouth, especially in public.

Some children become very attached to a blanket, muslin or soft toy. The special comforter, like thumb sucking, is often used to help the baby or child get to sleep by himself or is used to calm him during times of distress. However, it can become a problem if the child becomes obsessive about it and insists on dragging the comforter everywhere.

Nose picking is another common habit that many parents find extremely irritating and the way some children dispose of the contents can leave even the most liberal parents feeling totally revolted. While the majority of these annoying habits disappear with age, the following guidelines suggest how to prevent bad habits from forming, modify existing ones and encourage good habits. With children over 18 months I find the use of a star chart invaluable. It can be a great incentive to help establish good habits. For the star chart to be effective it is important that there are enough tasks on the chart in order for the child to achieve some stars every day.

Thumb sucking

All babies are born with a basic instinct to suck and nearly all babies will suck their thumb at some stage. Many start while in the womb, but it is not until a baby reaches almost three months that he will have sufficient hand-to-mouth co-ordination to keep his thumb in his mouth for any length of time. Once the baby has developed the necessary co-ordination for thumb sucking, how often he will do it and for how long varies considerably from baby to baby. The majority of young babies who suck their thumb do so either when tired, when using it as a comforter prior to sleep, or when hungry. Thumb sucking or hand chewing usually peaks between the ages of six and nine months with the need to suck gradually decreasing by the age of one year. While some babies continue to suck their thumb at bedtime, a baby who is continually sucking his thumb throughout the day is likely to develop a long-term habit that will be difficult to break.

If your baby is approaching a year old and is constantly sucking his thumb during the day, the cause is probably boredom. The best way to deal with this is to encourage more physical activity such as Tumble Tots or a swimming class. When at home, encourage more crawling or pushing of his baby walker and remember to rotate his toys so that he doesn't get bored. Distraction is much better than disapproval. Making a fuss about thumb sucking or constantly pulling his thumb out of his mouth rarely works and usually makes the baby or toddler more anxious, which increases his need to suck even more.

With older children excessive sucking may become a real problem as it can cause deformities of the teeth and jaw, resulting in extensive dental treatment. Again, disapproval of the habit rarely works; it is much better to work out the cause. Boredom, tiredness and insecurity are usually the main reasons. I often find that suggesting to an older child that he is tired and perhaps should go and have a rest in his room where he can suck his thumb in private immediately encourages him to find something better to do.

Dummies

As I have discussed, sucking is one of a baby's most basic instincts and some babies are more prone to sucking than others. If I find I have a particularly 'sucky' baby I actively encourage the use of a dummy rather than the thumb in the first few months. Over the years, I have observed that my sucky babies who were given dummies as a comfort during the first few months of their lives were less likely to develop a long-term thumb-sucking habit. The majority of my babies who were very sucky and not allowed dummies have developed long-term thumb sucking problems and some of them will definitely need corrective dental treatment. Most dentists would also agree that excessive day-time thumb sucking is much more likely to cause problems than sucking on a dummy.

If used with discretion a dummy can be an asset in the first few months. Unfortunately, it can also be a major cause of sleeplessness. A baby who is allowed to fall asleep with the dummy in his mouth can end up waking several times a night and refuse to settle back to sleep without the dummy. If I use a dummy to settle a baby I always remove it before he gets into a deep sleep even if it means he cries for a short period. I have found the majority of my babies wean themselves off the dummy somewhere between two and four months. If a baby doesn't show signs of abandoning it by four months I would get rid of it anyway, before he forms a long-term dependence.

Some parents are concerned about research done a few years ago claiming that babies who used dummies were found to have a slightly lower IQ. As the research was carried out on people who were in their 70s, it is debatable how accurate the records are. I have certainly not found that my babies who were given dummies are growing up any less intelligent than the ones who weren't.

If you decide to use a dummy for your baby it is worthwhile to consider the following points.

- If a baby is happy and content without a dummy, there is little point in introducing one in the hope that it will avoid thumb sucking.

- A sucky baby is one who, despite enjoying a full feed, keeps trying to get his thumb into his mouth and will fuss and fret until his sucking needs are met. Distraction and cuddling rarely satisfy the need for extra sucking with young babies under three months. If you decide to use a dummy, be selective as to when you use it.

- Allowing a baby to fall asleep with a dummy in his mouth can lead to very serious sleeping problems. Remove it before he falls into a deep sleep. It is better to have ten minutes of crying in the early days than the hours it will take later on to wean an older and more dependent baby off its use.

- Care should be taken when giving a breast-fed baby a dummy as overuse could interfere with the baby's desire to suck, which helps establish a good milk supply.

- Particular care must be taken to ensure that dummies are thoroughly washed and sterilised before being given to the baby. Poor hygiene when using a dummy can result in the baby getting thrush.

- The dummy should be taken away by the time the baby reaches four months, otherwise a long-term dependency may arise.

Dummies: giving up

In my experience, if a dummy has been used with discretion and the baby has not been allowed to fall asleep sucking on it, he will usually begin to lose interest in it somewhere between eight and twelve weeks.

Occasionally, I do have a baby who shows no signs of giving it up of his own accord, in which case I would gradually restrict the times I offer the dummy. Once solids are introduced I would take it away completely. Sometimes it results in the baby being fussy for a couple of days but I find that very young babies very quickly forget about the dummy.

With an older baby or child, getting rid of it can be a real problem, especially if they have been allowed to use it as a comfort to get to sleep. I have tried gradually restricting its use but have found it is better just to go 'cold turkey'. Trying to wean gradually very rarely works as the constant whingeing over several hours wears you into submission.

Comforters

Between six and nine months nearly all babies begin to develop an attachment to a comforter. The choice of comforter varies from baby to baby. Some become dependent on a blanket or muslin, others may choose a soft toy, use their thumb or a dummy. Psychologists believe this use of a comforter occurs around the same age that babies realize they are an individual person, separate from their mother. These transitional comfort objects give a baby or toddler a sense of security when they feel alone or vulnerable. Baby and childcare expert, Penelope Leach, says that a cuddly is thought to be a 'stand-in' for the mother as a comfort object, which the baby or child can use when that comfort is not available to him.

The majority of experts agree that use of a comforter is a normal part of a baby's development, but most stress the importance of a child not becoming overdependent on it. This can easily be avoided if comforters are restricted to rest times and sleep times. Allowing a baby to drag a muslin, blanket or toy around everywhere can lead to disaster if the item in question gets lost.

By three years of age most children become less reliant on their comforter and have usually abandoned it altogether by the time they reach five years.

The following guidelines can help avoid overdependency, which can lead to problems later on.

- When you notice your baby or toddler becoming attached to a certain object, limit its use to bedtime or special rest time in the house. Do not allow him to drag it from room to room or on trips out but obviously you would need to take it on holiday or for overnight visits. Otherwise be insistent that the blanket, muslin or toy stays in the cot.
- If possible try to purchase a duplicate, as this will allow frequent washing and provide you with a replacement if it becomes damaged or lost.
- If you find that your young baby or toddler is getting more and more dependent on a comforter and is withdrawn and not interacting like he used to, there could be some underlying emotional reason.

Nail biting

Nail biting should be treated in much the same way as thumb sucking. It is better to distract the child than to reprimand him. If a child's nail biting is being caused by anxiety, making a fuss about the habit will only make him more anxious and inclined to bite his nails. Finding out what is causing his anxiety and resolving the problem will often help eliminate this habit.

For the majority of children, nail biting is nothing more than a habit they will eventually outgrow. Some parents try painting their children's fingernails with a bitter tasting solution, but I have never known this approach to be very successful.

I have had some degree of success using a star chart. The child is encouraged to give up biting one nail at a time and for each day he doesn't bite that particular nail, he gets a star. It is important that no mention is made of the other nails he has bitten. At the end of the week, depending on how many stars he has on the chart, he will get a small present. If he has managed to go one week without biting that particular nail, I would then encourage him to give up biting a second nail. This very gradual approach can take a while but it does puts less pressure on the child. Often the appearance of a few unbitten nails is enough encouragement for some children to give up the habit completely. It is important to file any rough edges regularly and to emphasise how well his unbitten nails look.

I also find encouraging him to massage them regularly with cream can be an incentive to take pride in his hands.

Dawdling

Dawdling is very common between the ages of two and three. It also coincides with the age when many toddlers start nursery. All too often I have witnessed the scene of fraught parents struggling to get their toddler fed, washed and dressed in time for school. The more the parents coax and cajole him to hurry up, the more he will dawdle. To avoid this habit turning mornings into a war zone it is important to set strict rules for the morning routine. Ideally, the pattern should be established long before the toddler starts nursery.

The first thing that must happen when your toddler awakes is that he gets washed and dressed. He should then immediately be given breakfast. Once breakfast is over he should be encouraged to get everything ready that he needs to take to school. As an incentive, tell him that once he has done all these things he will be allowed 15 minutes to play, read a book or watch a video.

It is essential that you are consistent and firm so that he learns what is expected of him in the morning. This is all part of teaching a toddler to take responsibility for himself. The star chart is also a great way to help enforce this behaviour in the morning.

Tidiness

Getting your toddler into the habit of tidying up from an early age will help avoid much conflict at a later stage. Toddlers can be encouraged to keep their toys and clothes tidy as soon as they are able to walk. They should also learn that they have to tidy one set of toys away before getting another set out. This is easier to implement if toys are stored in different categories, in boxes with secure lids. This storage system also helps the toddler to define size, shape and colour. The cars belong in the long red box, the jigsaws belong in the tall green box and the crayons belong in the small round yellow box. While a large toy chest may be attractive to look at, I feel they are best avoided as they do little to encourage tidiness.

Teeth cleaning

Until your child has several teeth it will probably be easier to use the specially designed gauze pads that are currently available. These pads will enable you to rub his teeth and gums gently, removing any plaque and keeping his mouth free of bacteria.

Once he has several teeth you can use a small milk-teeth toothbrush. Choose one that has soft-ended bristles and a chunky ribbed handle, making it easier for your baby or toddler to hold. To begin with, most babies and toddlers are more interested in chewing the brush than in actually brushing their teeth. It is not until a child reaches six or seven years that he will begin to clean his teeth properly; until then he will need your help. Try to make cleaning his teeth fun. Play a game of Mummy's turn – your turn. With children under three it is usually easier to clean their teeth just before they get out of the bath, which avoids having to worry about dribbling.

The following guidelines will ensure that you establish the right habits for healthy teeth.

- It is important to use a toothpaste suitable for milk teeth that contains the correct level of fluoride and is sugar free. Using a toothpaste that contains too much fluoride can result in white specks on permanent teeth. A small pea-sized blob of tooth-paste is all that is needed.
- Ensure that your child's teeth are brushed at least twice a day. This will ensure that they are protected by the fluoride that stays in the mouth up to five hours after brushing.
- Always ensure that the toothbrush is rinsed thoroughly under hot water after each use and that it is stood upright to dry. It should be replaced every two months.
- Fruit juice and sugar-based drinks should be given with meals, not between meals. Acidic juices can damage the soft surface of children's teeth so choose non-acidic ones. By the time a child reaches a year old he should be having all drinks from a cup or beaker.
- Babies who are still being settled at bedtime with a bottle of milk are more likely to suffer from tooth decay, which can affect the permanent teeth that have not yet come through.
- Get your toddler used to visiting the dentist before he reaches 18 months. The younger he is when he visits, the less likely he is to feel intimidated. Try to choose a practice that specialises in children's dentistry.
- Once a toddler reaches the dawdling stage it is worthwhile investing in a Toothbrush Timer Set. This comprises a junior toothbrush and novelty stand that incorporates a timer. Rewarding the child with a star if he finishes brushing his teeth within the allocated time can be a great incentive.

Hands and nails

Once your baby starts on solids you should get into the habit of washing his hands before and after meals. When he starts walking you can begin teaching him how to wash his hands at the sink. By the time they reach two and a half the majority of children are capable of washing their hands by themselves although they will need supervision when filling the sink and help with drying their hands properly. Never leave your toddler unsupervised if he is able to turn on the hot water tap by himself.

To encourage good hand-washing habits, fill a small plastic container with novelty soaps and nail brushes and animal shape sponges used for painting. Most children find it more fun to soap the novelty sponge or nailbrush, then wash their hands with it. Drying hands will be made easier for the toddler if he uses a face-cloth rather than a towel. Choose one with his favourite cartoon character on it and hang it on a small hook at a height that makes it easy for him to reach.

Hands should be washed before and after meals and after a visit to the loo. They should also be washed on return from an outing or from playing outside and after handling pets.

It is also important to keep your baby's or toddler's fingernails short and clean. This is easy with very young babies as nails can be cut when they are asleep. With toddlers it can be more difficult as most hate having their nails cut. I usually find they are less likely to protest if allowed to watch a video while their nails are cut. I'm afraid this is the one time I usually resort to bribery.

Hair washing

A great many of the toddlers I know hate having their hair washed and will scream blue murder throughout the process. There is a specially designed shampoo shield that you can put on the child's head to reduce the chances of water getting in their eyes, but the majority of parents who have purchased this tell me that they make little or no difference to the child's screaming. The best advice seems to be to ignore the screams and forge ahead as quickly as possible. The sooner hair washing is finished, the sooner the screaming will stop.

Dressing

By the time they reach 18 months, most toddlers are capable of taking off some of their clothes. There are specially designed toys and dolls with buttons, zippers and press studs that can help them develop their manipulation skills. Even a very small child is capable of dropping his clothes in the wash basket and helping to lay out his clothes for the following day.

Between two and two and a half years the majority of children manage to remove all their clothes. Most are also capable of dressing themselves but may need help with buttons, braces and zips. Encouraging your toddler to master these skills will help develop confidence and independence. Also, the more skills your toddler learns before a second baby comes along, the easier it will be for you to cope when you have to divide your time between two.

Rocking and head-banging

Between six and twelve months some babies get into a habit of getting up on all fours and rocking their head back and forth. Others lie on their back and roll their head from side to side. This usually happens when they are tired or about to go to sleep. Occasionally, a baby may even bang his head continuously against the cot spars until he falls sleep. This rhythmic behaviour can be very upsetting for parents because it is often associated with children who are emotionally disturbed.

If your baby only displays this behaviour when he is tired and ready to go to sleep, there is very little to worry about. He is using these rhythmic movements to comfort himself. However, if he appears unhappy, fretful and displays this behaviour when awake, it would be advisable to seek advice from your doctor or health visitor.

Nose-picking

Many of the childcare books I have read say that nose picking is often done out of boredom or when the child is stressed. While this may be the case with some children, I believe the main reason is because the majority of children are not capable of blowing their noses until they reach three to four years of age. It is inevitable that a toddler will clear his nose of any irritating mucous the only way he can – by picking it.

Once your toddler reaches two or three years of age you can help him to learn how to blow his nose by demonstrating how to close one nostril while blowing down the other.

Like the majority of annoying habits, nose picking disappears with time. It is pointless reprimanding the child for picking his nose but he should be reminded it is something he should do in private.

Stammering

Stammering is very common between the ages of two and three years. It is also around this age that a toddler's vocabulary rapidly increases to 200 words or more. Therefore it is hardly surprising that a great many toddlers experience difficulty in articulating some words. Avoid becoming obsessed with your child's pronunciation by constantly making him repeat words correctly, it will only make him feel more self-conscious and tense. In my experience a toddler who becomes anxious and tense will be more likely to stutter or stammer. The majority of children will lose the habit of stammering by the time they reach four or five years, but if you have serious concerns about your child's speech development, you should discuss it with your doctor or health visitor.

Whingeing

All toddlers go through stages of being whingey. I have found that toddlers who were fussy and demanding as babies and never learned to entertain themselves are more inclined to develop a habit of whingeing. If you think your toddler's whingeing is becoming a serious habit, it is advisable to deal with it sooner rather than later. A child who is constantly whingeing and demanding will soon become very unpopular. The most effective way of dealing with a child who is whingeing is to sit him down and in a very serious manner explain that you cannot understand what he is saying when he speaks in a whiney voice. Tell him he must speak properly if he wants you to listen.

Thereafter when he whinges, say very simply and very firmly, 'I can't hear you', then walk away. It is imperative not to become involved in any sort of conversation whatsoever until he speaks properly. The reason he is whingeing in the first place is to get your attention. If he learns that you will totally ignore any whingeing, he will soon stop.

Private parts

Many parents get very concerned when their baby or toddler begins to explore and play with his private parts. A young baby will discover his genitals in much the same way as he does his mouth, hands and feet and many babies derive some pleasure from rubbing them. This behaviour was more noticeable when babies used to sleep on their tummies. I have observed babies as young as six weeks vigorously rocking and rubbing themselves in a rhythmical movement against the mattress. The pleasure that this action brings a young baby is more self-comforting and not at all sexual. If your baby develops this totally normal and unconscious habit it is best just to ignore it.

Once a toddler is out of nappies the interest in his genitals becomes more obvious. If your toddler gets into a habit of playing with his private parts it is important that you do not scold him or make him feel bad about his body. However, it would be advisable to teach him that some things are best done in private.

7

Freedom from frustration

By the time a toddler reaches his second birthday his walking will be much steadier and he will become more daring physically as he attempts to run, climb and jump. He will also become less frustrated mentally, as he able to communicate his needs better as he begins to string words together. However, during the third year he will be faced with a whole host of new challenges and helping to build his self-esteem will give him the confidence to deal with these challenges. They will include forming friendships with other children and learning how to share; starting nursery school and taking instruction in a group situation; learning good manners and respect for others; taking more responsibility for his own actions.

During this stage of development it is important that parents teach their child how to think and do not think for him.

Self-esteem and confidence

While it is important to teach a child to be cautious of certain things (ie the busy road, the steep stairs etc) parents should be careful not to overprotect their child so much that he loses his natural instinct to explore and the courage to try new things.

We have all watched children in the playground as they line up to climb the steps of the slide; one by one they slide down, squealing with delight as they do so. But in nearly every line-up there is the nervous child who climbs the steps extra carefully and very slowly, repeatedly looking back for a nod of reassurance from an all-too-often anxious parent.

This type of parent often seems to take great pride in announcing their child's fear to the world. 'He's such a sensitive little boy, so careful and cautious.' In reality it is often the parent who is over cautious, worried, anxious and fearful that their child should come to harm. A child who is constantly reminded to be careful when he attempts the everyday challenges all children face, will quickly lose the confidence and the courage to try different things and learn new skills.

Parents who constantly correct everything their child says or does can also damage their child's self-esteem. The desire for their child to achieve success in everything he attempts to do leads some parents to re-arrange the farmyard properly, finish off the edges of the colouring correctly, and more often than not frequently answer or finish a sentence for the child when he is asked a question. Their drive for perfection very quickly cripples his natural ability to try things for himself. He then becomes too anxious to try anything for fear of getting it wrong – frightened of disapproval.

The following guidelines give suggestions to help build your child's self-esteem and confidence.

- The way a parent helps their child approach the many challenges he faces has a great influence on how successful he will be in mastering the challenge. All too often I hear parents express concern that their child is bound to be like them and be frightened of heights, have no sense of balance, dislike dogs etc. A child is not a carbon copy of his parents, therefore it is very important that you do not assume that your child's strengths and weaknesses will be the same as your own.

- Between two and three years of age a child is becoming very aware of being a separate person and is beginning to form views and opinions of his own. It is very important that you allow your child time to think and answer for himself when asked a question.

- During the third year all children are capable of self-feeding, undressing and, apart from buttons and zips, dressing them-selves. Continuing to do these things for your child because it is quicker will do little to help his growing independence. Allow extra time at mealtimes and in the morning and evening so you have the patience to guide him and encourage him to do these things for himself.

- When teaching new skills it is important that you choose a time when your child is not overtired or hungry. Then, before doing it together, show him several times how it is done. Once he attempts it by himself it is important to praise him for his efforts even if he doesn't get it quite right.

- Second children appear to learn many skills much quicker, probably because they copy their elder brother or sister. An only child will benefit greatly from being given the opportunity to mix with other children at playgroups or if parents arrange play dates at home.

- It is important not to undermine your child's attempts at something new by comparing him with others. The length of time a child takes to learn a new skill varies for each child and the most important thing is that your child enjoys learning the new skill, not how long he takes to learn it. If you are concerned about your child's development it is better to talk to your health visitor than to worry unnecessarily.

- Learning a new skill requires a lot of concentration from a child, which can sometimes lead to frustration and anger. If, despite being shown several times, your child is still struggling with a new task, a difficult jigsaw or game, try to resist interfering or doing it for him. It is much better to defuse the situation by suggesting a rest period with a drink and a biscuit. Once he has calmed down and is relaxed he will be much more likely to listen to your advice on how to tackle the task.

During the third year most parents work hard to help build their child's self-esteem and to encourage him to become more confident. However, sometimes a child's increasing independence can cause him to become overconfident which can lead to disobedience. I think it is essential that parents strike a happy balance between encouraging their child's new-found confidence and teaching them that there are certain rules to which we must all adhere.

Obedience

Obedience, like the word 'discipline' will for many parents conjure up images of harshness and severity. During the second year allowances are made for the toddler because he has no real concept of right or wrong. However, as the toddler enters his third year nearly all parents expect some degree of obedience, and for many parents getting their toddler to do what he is told can become a real problem. Simple and reasonable requests such as 'clear your toys away', 'let's go upstairs for your bath', or 'take off your clothes' are all met with total resistance, and a battle of wills between parent and toddler usually ends up with him in tears, and being accused of being naughty and 'disobedient'.

Jane Nelson says 'a misbehaving child is a discouraged child, and we are more effective in redirecting the misbehaviour to positive behaviour when we remember the hidden message behind the behaviour. The misbehaving child is letting us know he does not think he has belonging and significance, and has mistaken beliefs about how to find belonging and significance.'

She suggests that the best way to help a misbehaving child is through encouragement. When discouragement is removed, the motivation for misbehaviour will be gone. She quotes Rudolph Dreikurs who helped develop Alderian psychology: 'Children are good perceivers, but poor interpreters'. Nelson explains this further by saying a child's behaviour will be based on what he believes to be true rather than on what is true.

I believe that much of the so called disobedience and bad behaviour of young children is caused by parents sending out confusing signals. Here are my suggestions for improving your child's behaviour.

- Dreikurs said that 'children need encouragement, just as plants need water. They cannot survive without it'. He believed that encouragement is one of the most important skills a parent can learn in helping their children. Try always to accentuate the positive and eliminate the negative by praising your child's good strengths, not his weaknesses. Expressing how pleased you are when he behaves well and reminding him of past times when he behaved well, will do more to encourage good behaviour than reminding him of the times when he misbehaved.
- Grandparents who indulge children with presents and special treats are one thing, but on matters such as behaviour and manners they should follow your rules, otherwise it will only lead to your child becoming confused and to conflict within the family. A happy, relaxed family environment with a clear

set of rules is more likely to result in a confident, well-behaved child, than an environment that is filled with tension and conflict.

- Lack of co-operation which results in bad behaviour is very often the result of the parents' inconsistency regarding rules and limits. For example, changing mealtimes and allowing later bedtimes to fit in with visitors or because Daddy is at home is bound to confuse a child under three years.

- Be realistic that the rules and limits you are setting are appropriate for your child's age and avoid having too many. Concentrate on getting your child's co-operation on important matters such as getting ready for bed, getting dressed, holding your hand in the street etc. Avoid rules that involve your child sitting quietly for lengthy periods; for example, it is unfair to expect a child under three years of age to sit quietly through lengthy adult lunches. Likewise, a child of this age can be encouraged to help tidy his toys and clothes away, but he is too young to be expected always to take the initiative to do so himself.

- Children learn very quickly that they are more likely to get away with bad behaviour in public. If your child misbehaves in a shop or restaurant or at a friend's house, no matter how embarrassed you feel, it is better to deal with disobedience in public the same way you would at home.

- Make sure your child has heard and understands your request properly. All too often parents shout across the room to small children that lunch or tea will be ready in five minutes, and get cross when the child, who is engrossed in playing a certain game, refuses to come when called at the forewarned time. It is better to interrupt his play for a few minutes and get down to his level so he can see the expression on your face and hear clearly what you are saying. Ask him to repeat back to you what it is you expect him to do in five minutes. Sometimes setting a kitchen timer to buzz in five minutes helps act as a reminder. Also the use of a star chart can be a very effective way of encouraging co-operation and good behaviour.

- A child over two years old who is constantly in the buggy or car and not getting enough exercise and fresh air is more likely to be boisterous, noisy and to get up to mischief around the home. All children benefit greatly from the opportunity to run in the fresh air every day.

During the second year much of the toddler's so-called disobedient behaviour can be put down to frustration and lack of understanding between right and wrong, therefore punishment is not an issue. However, during the third year the child is beginning to have a greater understanding of what is expected of him and the difference between acceptable behaviour and unacceptable behaviour.

A parent who gets the balance right between building self-esteem, encouraging independence and teaching their child obedience should rarely have to resort to punishing their child. However, rare as these times are, it is important for parents to have discussed and mutually agreed in advance how bad behaviour should be dealt with.

Punishment

All parents at some stage have to decide on appropriate punishments for the times that their child has been deliberately disobedient. Parents who are in disagreement over standards of behaviour and forms of punishment send conflicting signals to their child as to what is acceptable and what isn't. In my experience, these parents usually end up with a very manipulative and spoilt child.

During the third year, the first step a child will take towards becoming more independent of his parents is to attend nursery school. A child who has not learnt to co-operate with his parents at home will have a much more difficult time adapting to nursery school and taking instruction from other adults. All children will, from time to time, test their parents by being deliberately naughty and some form of punishment may be needed. Twenty years ago a quick sharp smack was considered as a fairly normal way of dealing with a disobedient child. Nowadays, childcare experts and parents are divided on whether smacking is an effective way of dealing with bad behaviour. Many child pyschologists believe that smacking a child leads him to believe that violence is the way to deal with situations he can't control.

Smacking is already illegal in Austria, Finland, Denmark, Germany, Norway and Sweden which should lead parents to consider seriously whether they should even consider it as a form of punishment

Smacking

In my experience, the majority of parents who resort to smacking their child do so when they feel they are losing control of a situation and their temper snaps. One of my clients who is totally opposed to smacking walloped her four-year-old son when he deliberately pushed his 18-month-old sister into the duck pond in Battersea Park, and another did the same when her three-year-old daughter ran into the middle of a busy London street bringing all the traffic to a screeching halt.

In both of these instances I can understand why the mothers resorted to smacking and agree with Christopher Green's belief that the minor emotional trauma caused by the smack is a small price to pay if it prevents the major pain of injury and keeps children alive and healthy. As he says, a hard smack might do more to engrave the message on a toddler's mind that climbing onto the edge of a high balcony is not allowed, than trying to debate democratically with him 'that it is rather dangerous as it is 50 metres onto the road below and he might sustain a nasty injury'.

Only a very few of my clients have ever resorted to smacking as a regular form of punishment for their children and it is my belief that as a punishment it rarely worked and only caused the children to behave more aggressively. I believe there are other methods of punishment that are far more effective than smacking. When deciding on a suitable form of punishment it is essential that the one you choose is appropriate. For example, with a child who throws his food on the floor or scribbles on the wall it would be better to make him clean the mess up than to make him take time out. Likewise the child who loses his temper and throws his toys around, should have the toys in question taken away for a short period. It is also important that the child is given a warning of how he will be punished should he continue to misbehave. A firm verbal warning given properly and in the right manner can often eliminate the need for any further punishment.

Verbal warning

When giving your child a verbal warning it is essential that you have his undivided attention. If he tries to run away from you it is important that you restrain him by sitting him down in a chair and holding his hands while you explain why you are unhappy with him. With children under 36 months it is important to keep explanations simple. All too often I hear parents getting more and more fraught as they get trapped into lengthy discussions with very young children of why something isn't acceptable. If there is a danger element attached to the misbehaviour then it certainly should be explained to the child why they mustn't do a certain thing. But for misdemeanours such as jumping on the furniture, throwing his books or clothes on the floor etc, it is sometimes easier to say something like 'Mummy doesn't do that, Daddy doesn't do that and Tommy mustn't do that'. Try to avoid statements like 'Tommy is naughty and he mustn't do that'.

The tone of your voice and the look on your face will play a huge part in whether the warning is effective. All too often I hear reprimands sounding more like requests, which have little or no effect on the misbehaving child. I believe that without resorting to shouting you do need to raise your voice slightly and that its tone along with the look in your eyes reflect how unhappy you are with your child's behaviour. A child must learn the consequence of his bad behaviour and it is important that you do not allow a verbal warning to turn into an empty threat. A child who is constantly threatened soon learns that his parents have no intention of punishing him and will soon become even more disobedient. If, despite giving your child a very firm warning, he continues to misbehave, the appropriate punishment should be administered immediately. Delaying the punishment for something he did several hours previously will only confuse him, as children under three years of age have not yet grasped the true concept of time. Once he has been punished, the bad behaviour and punishment should not be mentioned again.

Constantly reminding a child of his bad behaviour and using words such as 'naughty', 'nasty', 'clumsy', 'stupid' or 'silly' etc will not improve his behaviour, and often leads to negative feelings about himself, causing him to be even more rebellious.

When a verbal reprimand does not have the desired effect, the two most effective punishments to choose from are either time out or withdrawal of a privilege. Whichever approach you take will depend very much on the age of your child and the reason for the bad behaviour.

Time out

In my experience, a short spell of time out is the most effective way of dealing with a child under three years of age who is misbehaving. Children of this age love to be on the move the whole time and in the company of others which is why a short spell of solitude is the quickest way to calm down a child whose behaviour is getting out of control. It also teaches a child the consequences of breaking the rules and teaches him to take responsibility for his own actions.

Childcare experts are in disagreement as to where time out should take place and many advise against using the bedroom in case the child comes to associate this room with punishment and fear, which could consequently cause sleep problems. It is often suggested that instead of the child's bedroom it is better to sit the child on the 'naughty' step or put them in the 'naughty' corner. In my experience this rarely works and I agree with Richard Ferber that the bedroom is the best place. As he points out in his book, 'If putting a toddler in his bedroom will put him off sleeping, then presumably putting him in the bathroom will put him off washing, the dining room off eating, the lounge off sitting, the kitchen off dishwashing and so on. I choose the bedroom because it is sufficiently soundproof and far enough away from the rest of the house to give both parties the space they need to calm down'.

A disobedient child who ignores a verbal warning should be taken to his bedroom immediately before things get totally out of control. Having decided on this course of action it is essential that you carry it out quickly and calmly. The child who protests and screams should, if necessary, be picked up and carried there. The sooner you get your child to his room and leave him there the quicker he will calm down and the less likely you will be to lose control yourself and resort to shouting, arguing or nagging which is what usually happens when parents keep trying to reason with a distraught and disobedient child.

The purpose of time out is to give your child the opportunity to calm down and realise how much more pleasurable life is when spent in the company of others and that bad behaviour in the company of others is not tolerated. Leaving him alone and reminding him that you will return the minute he has calmed down is the quickest way to achieve this. However, I do not think there is any great benefit in leaving a small child upset and alone for lengthy periods, as it usually results in the child becoming hysterical and trashing the room. I would allow a period of between three and five minutes and if he hadn't calmed down I would return to the room and remind him that he would be allowed out if he was ready to behave. The answer is nearly always 'yes', therefore I would bring him out, but should he start misbehaving again I would repeat the whole procedure. With some children the procedure has to be repeated many, many times, but eventually they learn that an ignored warning of bad behaviour will always result in them being taken to their room.

Withdrawal of privileges

A simplified version of withdrawal of privileges can be used as the child gets nearer his third birthday. Because a child of this age still does not have enough awareness of time the withdrawal of the privilege must happen immediately. Restricting a video in the evening or cancelling a trip to the playground in the afternoon because he misbehaved in the morning will not be effective. However, there are certain occasions when a child is misbehaving that an immediate withdrawal of a privilege can work. For example, a child who is deliberately being destructive with a toy or book, or who scribbles all over the kitchen table should have the item in question removed for the remainder of the day. Likewise the child who insists on running around while eating a biscuit should have the biscuit taken away, and the child who misbehaves at a play date can be taken home.

As with time out the child should always be given a verbal warning of what will happen if he continues to misbehave. If you find you are constantly having to reprimand or punish your child for deliberate misbehaviour it is essential that you look closely at both the reasons for the misbehaviour and at the form of punishments you are using. It is also worthwhile discussing any worries you may have about your child's behaviour with your health visitor who will be able to reassure you as to whether or not your concerns have any foundation.

Gemma: aged twenty-seven months

Lucinda, mother of Gemma aged twenty-seven months and George aged three months, was at breaking point when she contacted me for help. She was finding it very difficult trying to cope with both children on her own (her husband left very early in the morning and often had to work late in the evening) and had become so depressed about the whole situation that her doctor had prescribed anti-depressants. I agreed to spend a week with the family to help put George into a routine.

On the evening of my arrival Lucinda explained her dilemma to me more fully. George was waking and feeding three or four times a night and fretful most of the day. While Gemma didn't wake in the middle of the night, she was difficult to settle at bedtime, often not falling asleep until 10 or 11pm. Since the arrival of her brother, Gemma had refused to take her midday nap, and was prone to several mega temper tantrums a day.

Although my role as a maternity nurse was to establish a feeding and sleeping routine for George, I felt so sorry for Lucinda that I suggested she have a complete break from both children, and take the whole of the following day off. I know that depression can make a problem appear much worse than it really is, and confidently assured Lucinda that I could easily cope with both children for one day.

The following morning after Gemma, George and I waved good-bye to a very anxious and worried looking Lucinda, I sat down and explained to my two angelic looking charges what an exciting day we were all going to have. Finger painting, colouring, cookie making and a picnic in the park were just a few of the activities I had planned.

By 5pm that evening I fully understood why on her departure that morning Lucinda had looked so anxious and worried. Within a few hours I had gone from being a calm, confident expert on childcare to a gibbering wreck. My plan for a day packed with enjoyable activities had ended up with the cream damask-covered sofa being covered in bright red paint. The colouring session ended up with Gemma trying to shove a jumbo green crayon into George's mouth, and during the picnic in the park Gemma somehow managed to get the lid off her any-way-up cup and drown George in apple juice. To protect George from

Gemma's frequent attacks, he was constantly carried and held, instead of the kicking under the play-gym that I usually recommend. Neither child had slept a wink during the day and by bathtime both were screaming hysterically. Trying to get them both upstairs that evening was a bit like trying to scale Mount Everest with two screeching baby chimpanzees attached to my back. My plans for structuring George's feeds had also gone out of the window as later that evening I counted no less than eight bottles of half-finished milk.

That night I made a silent vow that no matter how desperate or depressed a mother was, I would never again offer to help out with the elder siblings of my babies. For the remainder of the week I concentrated on structuring George's feeding and sleeping problems, and by the end of the week he was in a brilliant routine, happy and content during the day and settling well at 7pm, feeding at 11pm and going through until 6.45am. However, from my observations of the struggle Lucinda was having trying to cope with Gemma's mega tantrums, the food fights at mealtimes and battles at bedtimes, I doubted that Lucinda would have the time and the energy needed to keep George in the routine.

This certainly proved to be true, as only days after my departure I received a hysterical telephone call from Lucinda, begging me to go back for a further week as George had started to wake up in the night again. Trying to be more tactful than usual, I explained to Lucinda that it really would be pointless because it wasn't George who had the problem. As far as babies went he was one of the least demanding ones I had cared for, but even very easy babies require time and attention if any sort of routine is to be maintained. This was impossible in her case because trying to cope with Gemma's demanding and difficult behaviour left her very little time for George.

The sobbing Lucinda became so hysterical and her pleading wore me down so much that I agreed to go back for a further week, on the one condition that we sort out Gemma's behaviour. So much for the vows never to get involved with a toddler.

That evening I sat down with both parents to discuss how best we could improve Gemma's behaviour problem. From the observations that I had made of Gemma the previous week it was my belief that one of the main causes was their inconsistent approach in dealing with Gemma's disobedience, particularly at mealtimes and bedtimes. The following pin-points the main causes of Gemma's extreme disobedience, and shows the suggestions I made to her parents to improve the situation.

Bedtimes

- *I believed that a major cause of Gemma's bad behaviour during the day was her very late bedtime. Recent research shows that children of Gemma's age who are getting less than ten hours sleep at night are more prone to aggressive or bad behaviour. I advised that Gemma's bedtime should be brought forward using the late bedtime plan on page 103. Over a two-week period her parents managed gradually to bring her bedtime forward until eventually she was happily settling at 7.30pm.*

- *Gemma's inconsistent bedtime routine was the main reason she ended up fighting sleep and going to bed late. The inconsistency stemmed from the fact that her parents each followed a different approach on putting her to bed. Two or three evenings a week Gemma's father managed to get home early to put her to bed and despite pleas from Lucinda, he would immediately on his return get involved with some boisterous activity or game with Gemma. When the time came for her bath Gemma would be so hyped up that her father had to invent another game to get her upstairs. He would pretend to be an aeroplane and with Gemma perched on his shoulder would run around the house before eventually running up the stairs to the bathroom. The fun and games would continue right through the bath and while Gemma was getting dressed. Although she was perfectly capable of getting herself dressed and undressed she would be running around so much that her father would end up doing it for her. All of this would take so long that it meant that Gemma was rarely in bed before 8.30pm. She would be so overexcited that she was unable to settle, demanding more and more stories, another drink of milk, or one last cuddle from Daddy. It could often take a further two hours before she would settle.*

  On the evenings that Lucinda was by herself, running around after tea and flying Gemma upstairs on her shoulders was a physical impossibility as she also had the baby to deal with. Gemma, expecting but not getting the same fun and games she had on the nights Daddy put her to bed, would soon resort to tears and tantrums to get her way. Bathtime and bedtime usually ended up with Gemma in tears and refusing to settle. Lucinda would become so stressed trying to cope with both children that she would also be in tears.

I wrote down the following list of guidelines that had to be followed every night regardless of which parent was putting Gemma to bed.

- There should be no boisterous games or activities after tea that would cause Gemma to become overexcited. The 15-minute time gap after tea and before the bath should be spent with either both parents or one of them encouraging and helping Gemma to get into the habit of tidying her toys away. The use of a star chart was used as an incentive to get Gemma to do this.
- When it was time to go upstairs for the bath Gemma was to be given two choices. She could hold either one of her parent's hands and climb the stairs quickly and quietly, for which she would receive a further star, or she would be carried up without fun or fuss and put in the cot while her parents went back down to get the baby. It was important that on the night both parents put the children to bed together they still used the same approach. Gemma was to be given a choice on which she had to make an immediate decision, without coaxing or cajoling. On the nights she tried to provoke her father into playing on the stairs, she had to be picked up immediately and without comment taken upstairs and put in her cot until the baby was also brought up.

  While the bath was being run Gemma was to be encouraged to undress herself and would receive a further star when she attempted to take off most of her clothes. If Gemma tidied her toys away, climbed the stairs quickly and attempted to undress, she would be allowed to put three stars on the chart that hung on her bedroom door. A total of three stars was rewarded with a treat of her being allowed to have special bubbles in her bath.

Mealtimes

- *Mealtimes were another major problem for Gemma's parents, but with this they did both take the same approach. When Gemma played up and refused to eat both parents would resort to spoon feeding her, which usually ended up with Gemma in tears as they forced spoonfuls of food down her throat. From my observations of Gemma at mealtimes it was obvious that being allowed to drink an excessive amount of juice in between meals and while eating was a major cause of her lack of appetite. That combined with the unrealistic amount of food her parents expected her to eat, resulted in constant battles at mealtimes. I advised her parents to restrict her juice intake to mealtimes only. It should then be very well diluted and not put on the table until she had eaten at least half of her food, and in between meals she should only be given water. I also suggested that they should put only the smallest amount of food on her plate; for example, half a chopped-up fish finger, served with one tiny diced potato, one floret of cauliflower and one teaspoonful of peas. She was then to be left alone in peace to eat this, with no coaxing or cajoling. Once she finished this she was to be allowed a small drink of very well-diluted juice before being offered another small selection of food. If she didn't eat well at one meal she was not to be allowed to fill up on snacks before the next one. While Gemma still continued to be faddy about certain foods, this approach led to a huge improvement in the total amount she would eat over several mealtimes. Seeing that Gemma could eat reasonable amounts at some mealtimes gave her parents the courage to leave her to decide on how much she should eat at individual meals.*

Routine

- *Lucinda thought she had done all the right things to prepare Gemma for the arrival of her baby brother and although she had anticipated some degree of jealousy after the birth she was not prepared for Gemma's unpredictable behaviour. At times she could be very loving towards the baby attempting to kiss and cuddle him, then suddenly for no apparent reason she would become very aggressive, trying to hit or scratch him. In my experience, this type of behaviour is more common when there is no set routine for a second baby. A baby who is fed on demand and carried from room to room in his Moses basket is bound to represent more of a threat to the elder child. Lucinda was constantly telling Gemma off for going too near the baby or for making too much noise when he was asleep.*

Once Lucinda began to stick rigidly to the routine I had set for George and put him to sleep at nap times in the nursery it made it easier for her to give Gemma individual attention on a regular basis. I also suggested that when Gemma went to touch the baby they encouraged her to tickle his feet, saying how much George liked the way she tickled his toes. This form of diverting Gemma's desire constantly to touch him, was much better than reprimanding her for trying to touch his head.

Within days of her parents following my advice Gemma was like a different child, happy during the day and settling well at bedtime. Her eating improved dramatically and she was no longer aggressive towards George. I believe that many of the jealousy problems could have been avoided if both parents had encouraged Gemma to learn more skills before the arrival of her brother. This would have encouraged her to be more independent and not so reliant on her mother. Lucinda had no close family at hand to help out with the children. Also I feel she would have found coping with two children easier if she had got Gemma used to attending a playgroup or nursery once or twice a week.

I believe that most children of between two and three years of age benefit enormously from attending a nursery school or organised playgroup as it teaches them how to share and participate in group activities. I find that children who have learned these two important skills are also more confident and independent and less likely to resent the arrival of a new baby brother or sister.

Nursery or playgroup

When deciding on a nursery or playgroup for your toddler it is worth spending time checking out and visiting several nurseries or playgroups to ensure that the one you choose is structured to meet your child's needs. Discuss in detail the school's discipline policy and whether they have regular parents evenings or newsletters. It is also important to ensure that your child is ready emotionally, mentally and physically to attend nursery school. In my experience, a child who is used to being left with someone other than his parents for short periods will adapt to nursery much better than a child who has been cared for exclusively by his parents. I would suggest that several months before your child is about to start nursery you get him used to being left for short spells with either another family member or a good friend. Gradually increase the time he spends with them until he is happy to be separated from you for a period of 3–4 hours.

I have also observed that children who have been overprotected by parents have more difficulty adapting to the structure and rules within a nursery school environment. If your child is constantly looking for reassurance or refuses to co-operate with simple requests, it would be advisable to concentrate more on building up his self-esteem and confidence, also establishing very firm rules and limits so he understands obedience. Starting nursery or play-group is a big step for a toddler, therefore the more you can do in the weeks prior to him starting the easier he will find it to adapt.

The following guidelines give further suggestions that will help make your child's start at nursery a happy time.

- Children of three years of age still have no concept of time, so avoid talking about it too far in advance. When the time gets closer it is worthwhile investing in some of the many story books available which describe what happens when a child starts nursery.
- Arranging regular play dates with one or two other children who will be or are already attending the same nursery school can make things easier for your child. If you do not already know any parents in the area ask the nursery school teacher if she can put you in touch with other parents who will be sending their child at the next term.
- Taking a child to nursery for the first time can be very emotional for some parents. Try not to let your child sense your anxiety when it comes to leaving him. The first few partings

can often be made easier if you arrange with another mother to drop your children off together. Some nurseries encourage parents to stay with the children for a short period during the first week. This works for some children and not for others, and is worth discussing in advance with your nursery school teacher.

- Children who start off by attending nursery only one or two mornings a week, and gradually build up the number of days, are less likely to experience nursery fatigue. A child who has cut his afternoon nap and begins to display signs of becoming very overtired by the evening may need to have a short nap introduced again on the days he attends nursery.

- A child who has learned practical skills like dressing, undressing and self-feeding, and is completely potty trained will have a greater sense of independence and more confidence, making it easier to adapt to nursery, than a toddler who still relies on his mother to help him with these things.

- The first term at nursery can be both physically and mentally exhausting for a child. To ensure that your child does not suffer from nursery fatigue or becomes overtired at bedtime try to ensure that you start his bedtime routine early enough. A child between two and three years who is still having a nap in the afternoon would still need to be in bed by 7.30pm. But a child who has dropped his nap altogether may need to be in bed by 7pm if he is to avoid becoming overtired. Remember overtiredness is the main cause of bedtime battles and middle of the night wakings.

- Make sure that you spend a short time on his return from nursery discussing what has happened during the morning, and which activities he has enjoyed most. Express how proud you are of his efforts to try new activities. If you notice that there are certain activities that he doesn't seem to enjoy, it would be advisable to discuss with his teacher what you can do at home to make these activities more pleasurable.

Fear of separation from his mother can still be very strong for a child during the third year. Following the above guidelines and making sure that your child is emotionally, mentally and physically prepared for playgroup or nursery will prevent this becoming a problem. However, you may find that your child does develop other fears when he first starts nursery. Fear of the dark and monsters are the two most common fears that children between two and three years experience.

Fear of the dark

During the third year even the most happy and confident child can develop a fear of the dark. A child who suddenly starts becoming fretful and frightened at bedtime and talking of monsters being in the room should be taken seriously. At this age he is still unable to comprehend the difference between what is real and what isn't, therefore telling him not to be silly and that monsters do not exist will be of no help. Dr Miriam Stoppard says, 'If your child is afraid of monsters or ghosts say that you are a parent who can do magical things to them. Say that you are able to blow them away and give a big blow.' I have found this sort of approach far more effective that trying to convince the child the monster doesn't exist. Giving your child a special magic toy that sits near the door to keep the monsters out can also be a successful way of eliminating a child's fears.

Some parents tell me that leaving a small plug-in light on until the child goes to sleep can also be reassuring. If a child starts to wake up frightened in the night or have nightmares it would be advisable to leave it on all night. This in my mind is better than leaving the door open. Problems can often arise when a second baby comes along if the elder child is used to having the door open, as they are more inclined to get up in the night if they hear their mother attending to the baby.

Nightmares

The majority of childcare experts claim that nightmares before the age of three years are very rare. In his book *Solve your Child's Sleep Problems*, Dr Richard Ferber appears to disagree with these claims. He says that 'dreams, and even nightmares, unquestionably do occur during the second year of life'. Ferber believes that nightmares are mainly a symptom of day-time emotional struggles. He says that 'although most nightmares do reflect emotional conflicts, in most cases neither the nightmares nor the conflicts are "abnormal". Rather, the normal emotional struggles associated with growing up are at times significant enough to lead to occasional nightmares.'

Having been woken in the middle of the night many times over the years, to the screams of the elder siblings of my babies, I would have to agree with Ferber's view. Nearly all of these children were between 18 months and three years, and those able to talk would, once calmed down, be able to describe the nightmare.

Although all the experts are in agreement that a child who has had a nightmare should immediately be comforted and reassured, opinion is divided on whether they can be controlled or not. Dr John Pearce, author of *The New Baby and Toddler Sleep Programme* believes that because nightmares occur in the lightest stages of sleep, they can often be controlled. He explains that because a child's imagination is more adaptable than an adult's, it is more open to suggestions. He advises that parents work out a plan on how to deal with the monster, ie making the monster fall into a hole, drown or get trapped in a cage.

I personally find that this approach works much better than trying to convince the child there isn't a monster. All too often I have heard a young child getting more and more upset as their parents insist on trying to convince them that the monster isn't real. This happens because a child under three years of age who wakes up frightened by a nightmare is not yet able to grasp the difference between dreaming and reality.

I have also observed that those elder siblings of my babies who have suffered from nightmares, nearly all had inconsistent bedtime routines or had previously suffered with sleeping problems. It is interesting that very few of the babies I have helped care for that were put into a routine from the very early days have ever suffered from nightmares,which leads me to believe that a consistent routine is as essential for older children as for babies.

The following will help give you a clearer understanding of nightmares and their possible causes, and also guidelines for dealing with them.

- Nightmares occur during the second half of the night when a child is in a REM sleep cycle, often referred to as the light sleep. The child will cry out during the nightmare, and once awake may take some time to return to sleep if he cannot be convinced there is nothing to be frightened about.

- Go to your child immediately to calm and reassure him. If he is old enough to explain his nightmare and wants to talk about it, listen sympathetically, but do not force him to give details. Try to use the same calm approach and soothing words each time. Once he has calmed down, tuck him up with a favourite toy and remind him you are just next door. If he says he is frightened of the dark, it would be advisable to plug in one of the very low voltage socket lights for reassurance.

- During the third year, the physical, mental and emotional demands on a child increase very rapidly. In order to cope with these it is essential he has a consistent bedtime routine at a regular time. I believe that children under three years of age can rarely cope with a bedtime any later than 7.30pm, especially once they are attending nursery school or have dropped their midday nap. In my experience children who have frequent late nights are much more likely to suffer from disturbed sleep.

- Overstimulation before bedtime nearly always ends up in tears when the parents lose their temper with a child who becomes overexcited and refuses to calm down. A child who has had to be reprimanded and goes to bed fretful will be much more likely to wake in the night. Keep things as calm and quiet as possible after the bath, discourage your child from running around and avoid any rough and tumble games.

- The majority of children under three years of age do not have a clear enough understanding of the difference between reality and fantasy, and the wrong type of bedtime story or video can be the cause of nightmares. Try to avoid stories and videos that involve violence. For example, stories like *Little Red Riding Hood* and *The Three Little Pigs* could certainly cause nightmares for a child with a vivid imagination. With a second or third child it may be necessary to stagger the bedtimes so he is not subjected to stories and videos that are not suitable for his age.

- The child who has been used to his mother's undivided attention can feel threatened if the arrival of a new baby results in a sudden change in his daily routine. It is important to try and organise the baby's feeding and sleeping so you have time to give him some undivided attention at certain times throughout the day. Also by making sure the baby is settled in bed at 6.30pm you will have the time to give him the extra reassurance he needs at bedtime.

- If your child starts to wake up regularly from nightmares it is worth keeping a diary of his daily activities, in particular writing down anything that appears to trigger anxiety or upset him. It is also worthwhile writing down the details of the nightmare. Sometimes a pattern emerges which links the daytime activities to the nightmare and pin-points the cause. For example, a child who is frightened of dogs may be prone to nightmares when he comes into contact with one. Likewise feeling intimidated by an aggressive child at playgroup may also be a trigger for disturbed sleep.
- If the nightmares become more frequent and continue for more than a few weeks it would be advisable to ask your doctor for a referral to a sleep clinic.

Sophie: aged 35 months

Sophie had slept through the night consistently since she was nine weeks old, apart from a few occasions when she was unwell. She was nearly three years when her brother was born, and it was about a month later that she started to have nightmares. She would wake up screaming every night, usually between 3am and 5am. Both parents would go immediately to reassure her the minute she started screaming, although it could actually take over an hour before they could get her to calm down. The nightmare was always the same – a big tiger was trying to get in the window. The more her parents tried to convince her that the tiger was in her dream, the more hysterical and adamant she became that the tiger was outside and trying to get to her.

The situation got worse when Sophie's screaming started to cause the baby to wake up for the second time in the night. Normally he would wake up around 2.30am, feed quickly and settle back to sleep around 3.15pm until 6.30am. We now had to cope with trying to settle him back to sleep again around 4.30–5.00am, after he was woken by Sophie's crying.

As my booking was soon coming to an end I was desperate to try and sort out the situation, knowing full well that it would be extemely tough on the parents if they had to attend to both the baby and Sophie in the night. I was also concerned that the exhaustion of trying to deal with Sophie in the night was causing a drop in her mother's milk supply, and suggested that I take Sophie's monitor for a couple of nights to give her mother a rest.

That night Sophie woke up screaming at 4.30am. I went straight to her to reassure her. I decided against trying to convince her that there wasn't a tiger as I noticed when her parents took this approach it only seemed to make her more hysterical. Instead I got her out of bed and took her to the window and asked her to show me where the tiger was. She pointed down to the bottom of the garden and said he was hiding behind the shed. I agreed with her that there was something there, but I was sure it was a big stripey kitten and not a tiger. I explained that his Mummy had specially chosen to leave him in our garden as she knew we would look after him while she went hunting for food. The growling noise she heard at the window was not actually a tiger but the kitten asking for a drink of milk.

Within minutes of telling Sophie this story she had calmed down and within ten minutes of my tucking her up in bed she was fast asleep.

The following morning Sophie had remembered everything we had talked about in the night and was keen to go looking for the kitten at the bottom of the garden. I explained that the kitten only visited at night when his mother went hunting, but we could go down to the shed and leave him a bowl of milk for his return that night. That night Sophie again woke up at 4am screaming, but settled within minutes of me reassuring her that it was only the kitten shouting 'thank-you' for his milk.

From then on the imaginary kitten became a real part of the Sophie's life and every evening she would put a bowl of milk out for him. The wakings in the night became fewer and fewer, and when reminded it was Tiger, the kitten, growling for his milk and not the fierce tiger, she would settle back to sleep within minutes. Within a couple of weeks the nightmares had stopped, although Sophie continued to put out the bowl of milk at night for the kitten for a further five months. Then one evening as her mother was pouring out the milk Sophie announced 'Mummy, you only have to put pretend milk in the bowl, Tiger's a pretend kitten not a real one!'

Night terrors

Night terrors are much rarer than nightmares and a child having a night terror will behave very differently from a child who is having a nightmare. It can be very frightening for parents the first time they witness their child having a night terror. Most parents find their child sitting bolt upright in bed screaming, eyes wide open and staring straight ahead as if witnessing something really horrific. Sometimes the screaming is accompanied by incoherent moaning and thrashing around, causing them to sweat so profusely that they appear to have a fever. Unlike the child who wakes up screaming after a nightmare and looks for comfort and reassurance, a screaming child having a night terror cannot be comforted. Although his eyes are wide open, most experts are in agreement that the child is still most definitely asleep and parents are advised to resist waking him.

The following guidelines give suggestions on how to deal with your child if he is suffering from night terrors.

- Night terrors occur during the non-REM sleep often referred to as the very deep sleep, usually within 1–4 hours of falling asleep. Night terrors usually last between ten and twenty minutes and provided the child is not woken up, he will settle back to sleep quickly once the terror is over.
- A child having a night terror is rarely aware of his parents' presence. Trying to calm your child down by cuddling him during a terror will probably make things worse. Unless he shows signs of wanting to be held, it is better to just stay close by so that if needed you can prevent him from injuring himself.
- As the terror is coming to an end your child will begin to calm down and relax; at this stage you can help to settle him down by tucking him in. Try to avoid waking him or, if he does wake, avoid asking him whether he has had a bad dream. In the morning it is better not to mention the terror as your child may get very upset being questioned about something of which he has no recollection.
- Dr Richard Ferber believes that with very young children the cause of night terrors is overtiredness. He advises that parents should ensure their child gets sufficient sleep, and if necessary

consider an earlier bedtime. He also emphasises the importance of a regular and consistent day-time routine.

- Some experts suggest that a child suffering from frequent night
terrors should be gently roused 10–15 minutes before the
terror usually occurs, then settled back to sleep within five
minutes. But other experts argue that this could lead to problems for some children if they wake up fully and refuse to go
back to sleep.

- Although most experts say that all children eventually grow
out of night terrors I think it would be advisable to discuss
things with your doctor if your child is having frequent night
terrors.

Daniel: aged 28 months

*Daniel had always slept well, going through the night at 12 weeks
and apart from one occasion when he had a cold he had never
woken in the night. Therefore I was very surprised when his
mother announced that at 29 months he had started to wake up
in the night. Having an extensive library of babycare books which
she could refer to, she very quickly realised that Daniel's waking
was caused by night terrors and not nightmares. He displayed all
the typical behaviour of night terrors that I have described above.
She followed the advice given by Penelope Leach in her book*
Baby and Child, *putting all the lights on in order to try and dispel
whatever images Daniel was seeing. She would use a soothing
voice and the same familiar words to try and calm him, but would
not attempt to wake him. Unfortunately, more often than not,
Daniel would work himself up into an even worse state, yelling
and screaming as he threw himself around the cot. When things
reached this stage she did as Leach advised and would wipe
Daniel's face with a warm, wet face cloth, which would wake him
up. Once awake Daniel would have no recollection of the night
terror, but became so awake that it would then take his mother a
further hour or so to settle him back to sleep. Daniel was a very
happy easygoing little boy, who ate a perfect diet, and was emotionally very well balanced. We discussed the problem many times
but simply couldn't fathom what was causing the terrors.*

*Many months later, on the first night of a five-day visit with the
family, I observed Daniel's night terrors first hand. I was con-*

vinced that turning on all the lights and trying to calm him down actually made matters worse as he became even more agitated. I referred to Dr Richard Ferber's book for his view on the best way to deal with night terrors. His advice was the opposite to that of Penelope Leach. He advises parents against trying to calm the child and suggested that the child should only be held if he recognises them. The episode should be allowed to run its course and once the child shows signs of relaxing and calming down he should be helped to lie back down and be tucked in. All this should be done without waking the child or talking to him.

Daniel's mother agreed to follow Ferber's advice the next time Daniel had a night terror. She would enter the room without turning the light on, leaving the door slightly open so there was just enough light to see him. She would sit by his cot to ensure that he didn't harm himself, but she wouldn't touch him or talk to him. The first night she did this Daniel sat up in his cot, eyes wide open, staring straight ahead, screaming and shouting incoherently for approximately six minutes, after which time he gave a big sigh and lay back down to sleep. The whole episode took approximately ten minutes instead of the usual hour or more. From then on Daniel's mother used the Ferber method each time he had a night terror, which was usually once or twice a week.

Ferber also says in his book that with children under six years overtiredness is the main cause of sleep terrors. I suggested to Daniel's parents that this may be the cause of his terrors. During my visit I had noticed that they had moved his bedtime from 7.30pm to nearer 9pm so that his mother could spend more time with him on her return from work. Because he was sleeping to 9am in the morning his parents were not convinced that this was the case. However, they agreed to keep a diary of the times he went to bed and the nights he was woken by night terrors. They also agreed to try putting him to bed earlier on the days that his mother didn't work. After a period of two weeks the notes showed that going to bed late for one night did not cause Daniel to have a night terror but two late nights in a row did result in him having one. From then on they made sure that Daniel never had more than one late bedtime a week and he has never had a night terror since.

Nightmares and night terrors are two of the most common sleeping problems experienced by children during their third year. If dealt with properly these problems can usually be eliminated very quickly, unlike the problem of early morning waking.

Early morning waking

Whether a child will be an early morning waker is very much dictated by what happens during the first year. I have found that children who as babies were put to bed late and did not have proper established naps during the day, are much more likely to become early morning wakers, expecting to start the day often as early as 5am.

Sometimes, however, it can also become a problem when a child who has always slept well is transferred from their cot to a bed, usually sometime during the third year. With a child who has always slept well the problem is much easier to solve than with children who, over a long period of time have got into the habit of waking. There are also some children who do need less sleep, so it is unrealistic to expect them sleep longer or to get angry with them. They can learn, however, that when they wake up they must wait quietly until you go and get them up. By being firm and consistent and never getting into a conversation with a child who wakes early I do believe that they can learn not to shout or fuss when they wake up. Remember, the aim is to get your child either to lie quietly in bed listening to a tape or to play quietly with his toys, not necessarily to go back to sleep. Whichever one he chooses to do it should be done in a dimly lit room; on no account should a big light be put on or the curtains opened. These two things should only be done when you go to get him up, as he will eventually learn that these two cues signal the start of the day.

The following guidelines give suggestions on how to deal with a child who is waking early.

- If your child is able to open his bedroom door it is worthwhile considering putting up a stairgate on the door. Once children learn that they are unable to get out of the room they are much more inclined to climb back into bed, especially if the room is very dark. Parents should remember that there is also a safety issue to consider when a young child is able to get out of his room and wander around the house. Many years ago, I came face to face one morning with a three year old at the top of the stairs holding his three-week-old sister in his arms. I had gone downstairs to get the formula and in the meantime the baby had woken up; because the toddler was able to open all the doors he had decided to go and give the baby a cuddle. I shudder to think what would have happend if he had attempted to go down the stairs while carrying the baby. From that day on I only took bookings where the families had stair-gates on both the baby's and the toddler's room doors.

- I believe that a very dark room is just as important for a toddler and young child as it is for a baby. To my knowledge not one of the 300 babies I have helped care for has ever got up before 7am. As they get older some may wake at 6–6.30am but the parents tell me that after a short spell of singing or chattering to themselves they usually go back to sleep until 7.30am. I am convinced that the reason this happens is because they are all used to sleeping in very dark rooms, with the door shut.

- If a child develops a fear of the dark he should not be forced to sleep in pitch darkness. It is much better to use a plug-in low voltage night light than to leave the door open as the latter encourages the child to get up, expecting to start the day.

- A child who wakes up before 6am and gets out of bed expecting to start the day should be put straight back to bed and told simply and firmly 'it's not time to get up yet'. It is important not to get into discussions of any sort. If you are consistent enough and follow it through no matter how often he gets out of bed, this method will eventually work. If he is in the habit of getting up and asking for a drink, make sure that a small beaker of water is always left by his bedside.

- Many parents claim that using a bunny alarm clock helps to prevent their child from expecting to start the day too early. The clock is designed to look like a bunny's face and has eyes that open and shut, which are operated by an alarm mechanism. At night the parents set the alarm for the time their child is allowed out of his room in the morning. The eyes of the bunny then shut and only open up again at the time for when they have set the alarm. I find that giving the child a star on his chart for the mornings he waited until the bunny's eyes opened before calling out can sometimes be a big incentive. However, I feel I should mention that some very determined children quickly learn how to operate the clock and manage to get the eyes open long before the time for when it was set!

- A child who is waking nearer 6.30am and getting out of bed should not be forced to go back to bed, but he can learn to play quietly in his room with his toys until the bunny's eyes open. Sometimes pre-setting a cassette recorder to play a nursery ryhme tape around the time the child usually wakes can encourage him to stay in his bed. Again, he can be rewarded with a star on his chart on the days he does remain quiet.

There are other problems that parents experience during the third year; lack of manners and not wanting to share are two things that the majority of parents are concerned about. All parents want their child to be polite and show kindness and sensitivity towards other people. Because children under three years are still very self-centred they will need constant reminders while learning these social skills.

Social skills

The more a child is taught to take responsibility for his own actions and the consequence of unacceptable behaviour, the easier it will be for him to learn to be polite and respectful of other's feelings. Many parents assume that their child will automatically turn out to be well mannered because they are well mannered themselves. The following guidelines give advice on how to encourage your child to be well mannered and respectful.

Please and thank-you

By the age of two years most children have a good comprehension of what is being said to them, even if their vocabulary is still fairly limited. It is important, therefore, that you ensure that you always remember to use these words yourself when talking to your child. During the first half of the third year your child will need constant reminders to say 'please' and 'thank-you', but as he gets nearer his third birthday he should need reminding less and less. If your child reaches three years of age and you are regularly having to say 'what's the magic word?' a different approach may be needed.

Completely ignoring the request of a child who forgets to say 'please' will quickly teach him to remember the magic word, likewise not letting go of something your child has asked for before he has said 'thank-you' will teach him the importance of these two words. During the third year you should also encourage your child to draw pictures which can be sent as thank-you letters for gifts he has received from family and friends or when he has attended birthday parties or other events.

Table manners

I believe that the majority of children will learn good table manners naturally if they are given the opportunity to eat with adults, provided of course that the adults themselves set a good example. A child who eats well and enjoys mealtimes will learn good table manners much quicker than the child who eats poorly. Trying to instill too many rules at one time about table manners can cause further eating problems for a child who is already eating poorly. Try to make mealtimes as happy and relaxed as possible and avoid possible distractions such as having the television on.

During the third year, eating becomes less messy and a child will have learnt that the throwing and spilling of food is unacceptable. While occasional mishaps of spilling or dropping food should be overlooked, a child who deliberately behaves like this should be reprimanded. However, reprimanding a child of this age for eating with his mouth open, not putting his cup down between sips or leaning his elbows on the table would be completely unreasonable.

While your child does need to learn the difference between good and bad table manners, it is unfair to expect him to be able to concentrate on learning all these skills at the same time so work on one skill at a time.

Interrupting

Teaching a child under three years of age that it is bad manners to interrupt you while you are having a conversation with a friend or talking on the phone is virtually impossible. As already discussed, before the age of three years children do not fully understand the concept of time and therefore can't grasp what waiting a few minutes really means. The majority of parents that I know with children of this age openly admit to bribery when they need to make an urgent phone call or have an important conversation with someone. Allowing their child to watch a video or giving a drink of juice and a biscuit usually guarantees ten minutes of uninterrupted conversation time.

Like the majority of social skills children learn best by example. Therefore approaching your child politely when you require his attention will go a long way towards helping him learn him how not to interrupt rudely.

Playing fairly

All parents want their children to grow up to be popular and well liked. A child who has learnt to compromise, play fairly and be considerate of the needs of others will be much more likely to achieve this than a child who only thinks of his own needs and refuses to share.

Sharing is something that all children have to learn and the best way to achieve this is to ensure that your child has regular opportunities to play with other children. Up to the age of two years children tend to spend much of their time playing alongside each other, not with each other. It is only during the third year that they begin to show signs of participating in play with other children. During this stage of development arranging short play dates with only one or two other children will make it easier for you to teach your child about sharing and taking turns. It is also easier to control things when there are fewer children, therefore avoiding tears and tantrums. Choose friends carefully, avoiding children who are aggressive and unruly. Sometimes it can be a good thing to invite a child who is slightly older and has learnt the importance of give-and-take while playing.

Prepare your child in advance by talking about and getting out the toys he thinks his friends would like to play with. If during the play date your child gets possessive about a particular toy another child is playing with, do not force him to give the toy back to the child. Instead take the other child aside and find him something special to play with. Young children hate being ignored and by doing so you will find your child is much more likely to offer to give the toy back, than if you try to force him to do so. When it comes to snack time encourage your child to offer the biscuits to his guests first, and remember always to express your pleasure and approval at the times when he shows consideration towards others. A star on his star chart on the days he has played nicely with his friends will also go a long way towards encouraging good behaviour.

Final note

I hope that the guidelines and suggestions given in this book will help you to avoid many of the common problems faced by parents during the first three years of a child's life. In my first book I repeatedly stressed the importance of parents structuring a baby's feeding and sleeping habits. My firm belief is that many of the problems experienced by parents of young babies are either food related or sleep related, and often both. I am convinced that this is also true of toddlers and young children. The case histories in this book and the thousands of phone calls and letters I have received since the publication of my first book confirms my beliefs that an overtired and poorly nourished child is far more likely to suffer from nightmares, tantrums, jealousy and aggressive behaviour than a child who is well rested and eats well.

I cannot stress enough, therefore, the importance of ensuring that your child continues to have a regular feeding and sleeping pattern. A regular routine along with your love, encouragement and lots of patience will go a long way towards helping him cope with the many challenges he faces during the first three years.

Useful addresses

Black out lining & roller blinds

Available from all John Lewis Partnership stores throughout the UK.

Breast pumps

Egnell Ameda Ltd
Unit 2, Belvedere Trading Estate
Taunton
Somerset TA1 1BH
Tel: 01823 336362
Fax: 01823 336364

Cotton sleeping bags

Kiddycare (Mail order)
Tel: 01309 674646
Fax: 01309 674646

Baby equipment

The Great Little Trading Company
124 Walcot Street
Bath BA1 5BG
Tel: 0990 673009
Fax: 0990 673010

Organisations

Foundation for the Study of Infant Deaths
14 Halkin Street, London SW1X 7DP
Tel: 0171 235 0965

Maternity nurse agencies

Nannies Incorporated
162–168 Regent Street
London W1R 5TB
Tel: 0207 437 8989
Fax: 0207 437 8889

For a personal telephone consultation with Gina Ford or details of her parenting classes, workshops and seminars in your area telephone: 01289 303351.

Or you can find her on her new website: www.contentedbaby.com

Gina would also like to hear from parents who are interested in forming local Contented Baby support groups in their area – for more details contact her on the above number.

Further reading

Ferber, Richard *Solve Your Child's Sleep Problems*, Dorling Kindersley 1986

Ford, Gina *The Contented Little Baby Book*, Vermilion 1999

Green, Christopher *Toddler Taming*, Vermilion 1992

Hollyer, Beatrice and Smith, Lucy *Sleep – The Secret of Problem-free Nights*, Ward Lock 1996

Jackson, Deborah *Three in a Bed*, Bloomsbury 1989

Jayachandra, C.R. *Screaming Babies*, J.C. Publications 1992

Leach, Penelope *Baby and Child*, Penguin Books 1989

Morse, Elizabeth *My Child Won't Eat*

Nelson, Jane *Positive Discipline*, Ballantine Books 1981

Pearce, John *The New Baby and Toddler Sleep Programme*, Vermilion 1999

Symon, Brian *Silent Nights*, Oxford University Press 1998

Stoppard, Miriam *The New Baby Care Book*, Dorling Kindersley 1990

Van de Rijt, and Plooij *Why They Cry*, Thorsons

Weissbluth, Marc *Healthy Sleep Habits, Happy Child*, Ballantine Books 1987

Index